THE AUSTRALIAN **Women's Weekly**

DESSERTS

THE AUSTRALIAN
Women's Weekly

DESSERTS

ACHIEVABLE, SATISFYING
SWEET TREATS

Project Editor Siobhán O'Connor
Project Designer Alison Shackleton
Editor Kiron Gill
Jacket Designer Alison Donovan
Jackets Coordinator Jasmin Lennie
Production Editor David Almond
Production Controller Denitsa Kenanska
Managing Editor Dawn Henderson
Managing Art Editor Alison Donovan
Art Director Maxine Pedliham
Publishing Director Katie Cowan

First published in Great Britain in 2022
by Dorling Kindersley Limited
DK, One Embassy Gardens, 8 Viaduct Gardens, London, SW11 7BW

The authorized representative in the EEA is Dorling Kindersley
Verlag GmbH. Arnulfstr. 124, 80636 Munich, Germany

A CIP catalogue record for this book is available from the British Library.
ISBN: 978-0-2415-4848-6

Printed and bound in China

For the curious
www.dk.com

MIX
Paper from
responsible sources
FSC™ C018179

This book was made with Forest Stewardship Council ™ certified paper –
one small step in DK's commitment to a sustainable future.
For more information go to www.dk.com/our-green-pledge

Contents

Desserts

For most of us today, desserts are treats to be relished when we're eating out, have guests over, or gather for a special family meal, rather than something we eat every day. All the more applause for the cook, then, when something sweet and beautiful appears to crown the meal.

The recipes in this book are innovative twists on classics. Some are simple and quick-to-put-together options, while others are more time-consuming – extravagant offerings to impress on a special occasion, but well worth the effort. With so many tempting choices, narrowing down what to make can be a conundrum for anyone with a sweet tooth. With this in mind, for ease we have grouped the recipes in the book according to flavour combinations, many of which have a seasonal bent, and a final chapter for special festive occasions, for those times when you want to pull out all the stops.

Fresh and fruity

In this chapter citrus, berries, passionfruit, and stone fruit all reign supreme, as well as more exotic fruit such as mango, figs, and pomegranate. It may seem that nothing could exceed the appeal of a perfectly ripe piece of fresh fruit – but, then, what about a luscious meringue stack filled with a tangy lemon passionfruit cream and topped with raspberries?

Let your choices be led by the fruit that is in season, as this will provide the best-tasting dessert. Embrace fruit that corresponds with cooking methods that suit the time of year too. In cooler months, seek out baked treats, such as satisfying apple, blackberry, and marzipan pies or a clafoutis of late-season berries, or enjoy the comfort that only a warm pudding can bring. If the sun is shining and the weather is warm, opt for something lighter and fresher. Granitas, cheesecakes, and meringues are all good choices and, like gelatine-based desserts such as panna cotta, have the distinct advantage of being able to be prepared well in advance.

Chocolate and coffee

These two ingredients conjure up tempting visions of richness and indulgence. Depending on the cooking method, the texture and intensity of flavour can be altered. A chocolate–egg base, lightened with egg whites, becomes a light-as-air soufflé. For lovers of rich chocolate desserts, we include a self-saucing pudding, fig-laden brownies, and the Spanish fried pastry churros, in which crisp lengths of pastry are unabashedly dipped in a molten chocolate sauce. Coffee and chocolate are good bedfellows, too, enhancing each other's flavour, so you will see them in company in this chapter as well as alone.

Nuts and caramel

With just eight nuts at your command, a world of possibilities opens. Nuts left whole and toasted provide texture within desserts, as well as adding depth to their flavour profile. Ground to a flour they make puddings, cakes, crumble toppings, and cookies that look marvellous but are surprisingly simple to make. Caramel is the alchemy that happens by cooking sugar and water to a burnished golden hue; the process of caramelization dissipates the sweetness of sugar, developing complex aromas and flavours that can be buttery, sour, nutty, malty, or toasty. Caramels that include butter and cream become butterscotch and add further richness and mouthfeel. Nuts and caramel can stand as sweet confections all on their own, too, such as crunchy cinnamon-spiced almonds or home-made caramels that range from simple fudge to more sophisticated caramel with intriguing flavour twists. Ready-made caramel sauces such as dulce de leche feature here, too, adding their own stamp in flavour and texture combinations designed to entice.

Spices and herbs

Spices and herbs have been making their way along spice and trade routes and into various cuisines since ancient times. Fragrant vanilla, the world's favourite flavouring, is of course used throughout the book, but you will find it united with other flavours such as basil, rosemary, and even chilli here. Infusing milk or cream-based puddings is another simple way to add interesting flavour notes. And spices are one of the easiest ways to add different sparks of flavour. Sweet treats with spices especially complement a menu with a Mediterranean or Middle Eastern bent.

Special occasions

One of the deepest pleasures of special festive times is the appearance of traditional treats that have become an essential and time-honoured part of the whole occasion. They may be treats that belong entirely to a particular festival or tradition, such as Christmas cake, or they may be things that appear at other times of the year but always mean the marking of an important occasion, such as a trifle. They may simply be a tradition closer to home, such as the special cake that is always baked for birthdays. All are treasured for what they mean beyond just the pleasure of eating them: continuity, togetherness, the assurance that some things never change. Or do they? Lots of people who celebrate Christmas will remember when that meant a hot plum pudding or fruit cake on the day – but the idea of having a frozen dessert or other pudding has caught on quickly, and today it has become a parallel tradition to the old ones. It's called enjoying the best of both worlds.

And so, the result is this beautiful collection of sweet treats and heady desserts. Go ahead and indulge – and impress yourself, your family, and your friends.

FRESH AND FRUITY

From delectable tarts and puddings bursting with flavour to frozen treats and cheesecakes perfect for the lazy days of summer, these desserts showcase the best of seasonal fruit.

Ruby red slab tart

BAKED AND FRESH | PREP + COOK TIME **45 MINUTES + REFRIGERATION** | SERVES **8**

A slab tart is an easy and not-at-all-intimidating tart for a novice baker, as it eliminates some of the elements that may cause grief. As an added bonus, it also requires no specific bakeware – a boon in the repertoire of any baker, regardless of skill level.

1⅓ cups (200g) plain flour

2 tbsp cocoa powder

2 tbsp icing sugar

150g chilled butter, chopped

about 2 tbsp iced water

300g coconut yogurt (see tips)

75g watermelon, peeled into thin slices

3 fresh figs (180g), cut into wedges

8 strawberries, halved

125g raspberries

1 tbsp pomegranate seeds (see tips)

glaze

1 cup (250ml) pomegranate juice

2 tbsp cranberry sauce

1 tbsp glucose syrup or honey

1 Preheat the oven to 180°C (160°C fan/350°F/Gas 4).

2 Pulse the flour, cocoa powder, icing sugar, and butter in a food processor until the mixture forms coarse crumbs. With the motor operating, add just enough of the iced water that the dough comes together. Turn onto a clean work surface. Shape into a rectangle. Wrap the dough in cling film. Refrigerate for 20 minutes.

3 Roll out the pastry between sheets of baking parchment into a 5mm thick 15cm x 30cm oval. Discard the top sheet of baking parchment. Transfer the pastry, still on the parchment, to an oven tray. Bake for 12 minutes or until cooked through. Allow to cool to room temperature.

4 Meanwhile, to make the pomegranate glaze, combine the ingredients in a small saucepan over a high heat. Bring to the boil. Boil for 10 minutes or until reduced to a syrupy consistency.

5 Spread the yogurt over the cooled pastry, leaving a 1cm border. Top with the fruit and pomegranate seeds. Drizzle with the pomegranate glaze.

TIPS

- To remove the seeds from a pomegranate, cut the pomegranate in half. Hold it, skin-side up, over a large, deep bowl. With a wooden spoon, tap the skin vigorously, squeezing the pomegranate half slightly, to release the seeds. Continue until all of the seeds are released, then remove any white pith that may have fallen into the bowl.
- Spread the tart with mascarpone instead of the coconut yogurt, if you like.
- To avoid the pastry softening, assemble the tart close to serving.

Lemon and passionfruit pavlova stack

BAKED/ASSEMBLAGE | PREP + COOK TIME **1 HOUR 45 MINUTES + COOLING** | SERVES **10**

This impressive-looking dessert is a meltingly light confection of crisp and soft meringue.
The lemon curd, raspberries, and passionfruit cut through the sweetness of the meringue,
lending freshness and acidity for a perfect balance of flavours.

6 egg whites

pinch of cream of tartar

1$\frac{1}{2}$ cups (330g) caster sugar

3 tsp cornflour, sifted

2 tsp vanilla bean paste

1$\frac{1}{2}$ tsp white vinegar

250g fresh raspberries

lemon passionfruit cream

600ml double cream

$\frac{2}{3}$ cup (160ml) lemon curd

$\frac{1}{2}$ cup (125ml) passionfruit pulp (see tips)

meringue cones

$\frac{3}{4}$ cup (165g) caster sugar

3 egg whites

TIPS

- If you're short on time, use premade meringue pavlova bases for the pavlova stack instead of making your own, and continue on from step 4.
- The pavlovas can be baked a day ahead; store in an airtight container in a cool, dry place.
- You will need about 6 passionfruit. Omit folding the passionfruit pulp through the cream, if you like, and spoon over the cream layers instead.
- The pavlovas are quite delicate. Use 2 large egg slices, metal spatulas, or the bases of loose-bottomed tart tins to lift and move them.
- This recipe is best assembled close to serving.

1 To make the pavlova bases, preheat the oven to 120°C (100°C fan/250°F/Gas $\frac{1}{2}$). Grease two 20cm springform cake tins and line the bottoms with baking parchment.

2 Using an electric mixer, whisk together the egg whites and cream of tartar until soft peaks form. Gradually add the sugar, beating after each addition, until the sugar has dissolved and the mixture is thick and glossy. Fold in the sifted cornflour, then the vanilla and vinegar.

3 Divide the meringue between the prepared tins; smooth the tops. Bake for 1 hour or until dry to the touch. Turn off the oven. Allow them to cool completely in the oven with the door ajar, before removing from the tins.

4 Meanwhile, to make the lemon passionfruit cream, using an electric mixer, whip the cream in a bowl until firm peaks form. Fold through the lemon curd and passionfruit pulp. Refrigerate until needed.

5 Carefully place 1 pavlova on a plate. Top with three-quarters of the lemon passionfruit cream. Sprinkle with half of the raspberries. Top with the remaining pavlova. Spoon over the remaining cream.

6 To make the meringue cones, stir the sugar and $\frac{1}{4}$ cup (60ml) water in a small saucepan over a low heat until the sugar dissolves. Increase the heat to high. Bring to the boil. Boil, without stirring, for 4 minutes or until the syrup reaches 118°C/244°F (soft-ball stage) on a sugar thermometer (or until a small amount of syrup dropped into ice-cold water can be rolled into a soft, pliable ball). Using an electric mixer, beat the egg whites in a bowl until soft peaks form. Gradually beat in the hot sugar syrup. Beat for a further 5 minutes or until cooled to room temperature.

7 Preheat an oven grill to a high heat. Using 2 tablespoons of mixture at a time, drop onto a baking tray, forming peaks. Grill for 30 seconds or until the meringue cones are lightly browned. Using a palette knife or egg slice, gently transfer the meringue cones onto the pavlova stack. Serve scattered with the remaining raspberries.

Roasted plums with rosewater

SET | PREP + COOK TIME **45 MINUTES** | SERVES **4**

Rosewater adds a touch of elegance to any dessert, and these plums are delightfully tender, sweet, and floral. Madeira cake has a denser texture than ordinary butter cake or sponge, making it easier to slice into cubes as in this recipe or for other desserts such as trifle.

6 small plums (450g), halved and quartered

1/2 cup (110g) caster sugar

1 tbsp rosewater

1 tsp vanilla bean paste

200g purchased Madeira cake, chopped into cubes (see tips)

50g butter, melted

1 cup (250ml) double cream

2 tbsp icing sugar

1/4 cup (35g) coarsely chopped pistachios

2 tbsp fresh raspberries, torn

1 tbsp unsprayed dried rose buds (optional)

1 Preheat the oven to 220°C (200°C fan/425°F/Gas 7).

2 Gently combine the plums, caster sugar, rosewater, and vanilla in a large bowl. Spoon the mixture into a shallow baking dish. Roast for 15 minutes or until tender, turning the plums halfway through the cooking time.

3 Meanwhile, combine the cake and butter in a medium bowl. Arrange the cake pieces in a single layer on a baking tray. Bake for 10 minutes, turning halfway through the cooking time, or until golden.

4 Using an electric mixer, beat together the cream and icing sugar in a medium bowl until soft peaks form.

5 Divide the cream among 4 serving bowls; drizzle with a little syrup from the plums. Top with the roasted plums, buttered cake pieces, pistachios, raspberries, and dried rose buds, if you like.

TIPS

- Use your favourite recipe for Madeira cake instead of buying ready-made, if you like. You will need to make the cake a day ahead.
- The roasted plums and buttered cake cubes can be prepared several hours ahead of serving.
- You could make this recipe with other stone fruit such as apricots or nectarines, if you like.
- Edible dried rose buds and petals are available from supermarkets and speciality food shops.

Coconut banana fritters

FRIED | PREP + COOK TIME **30 MINUTES** | SERVES **4**

Using panko breadcrumbs instead of regular breadcrumbs or simple crushed-up biscuits
ensures these fritters have an extra crunchy shell to bite into when you eat them. The textural
sensation provides a wonderful contrast to the softness of the banana in the middle.

1/4 cup (40g) icing sugar

2 tsp ground cinnamon

1 egg

3/4 cup (50g) panko breadcrumbs

1/4 cup (20g) shredded coconut

vegetable oil for deep-frying

4 large bananas (920g), halved lengthways

2 cups (500ml) coconut ice cream (see tips)

1 Combine the icing sugar and cinnamon in a shallow bowl. Lightly whisk the egg in another shallow bowl. Combine the breadcrumbs and coconut in a third shallow bowl.

2 Fill a large saucepan or wok with vegetable oil until it is one-third full. Heat to 180°C/350°F (or until a cube of bread dropped into the oil sizzles and browns in 15 seconds).

3 To make the fritters, dip the bananas first in the icing sugar mixture; shake off any excess. Next, dip in the egg mixture, then lastly in the crumb mixture to coat. Deep-fry the bananas, in batches, for 2 minutes or until the coating is golden. Drain on kitchen paper.

4 Serve the hot fritters with scoops of the ice cream.

TIPS

- To make your own coconut ice cream, soften 2 cups (500ml) good-quality vanilla ice cream, then fold in 1/2 cup (35g) toasted shredded coconut and 1 tbsp coconut-flavoured liqueur or 1/2 teaspoon coconut essence. Return to the freezer until firm enough to scoop.
- You can use coconut yogurt instead of the ice cream, if you like.

Strawberry jellies with snowballs

FRESH AND FROZEN | PREP + COOK TIME **1 HOUR 10 MINUTES + REFRIGERATION + FREEZING** | MAKES **6**

This is a perfect summery dessert to celebrate the start of the strawberry season – a grown-up version of jelly and ice cream. Choose the ripest, most fragrant strawberries you can find, to make the most of this double infusion of their heavenly flavour.

1kg strawberries, thinly sliced

²/₃ cup (150g) caster sugar

¹/₃ cup (80ml) Pimm's No. 1 Cup

8 small gelatine leaves (13g)

2 cups (500ml) vanilla ice cream

50g purchased meringue nests, crushed

2 tsp dried pink peppercorns, crushed (optional)

macerated strawberries

250g fresh strawberries, sliced 3mm thick

1 tbsp caster sugar

2 tsp lemon juice

1 Put the strawberries, sugar, and Pimm's in a large heatproof bowl. Cover tightly with 2 layers of cling film. Place the bowl over a large saucepan of simmering water. Heat for 40 minutes.

2 Place a large fine sieve over a large jug or bowl. Strain the strawberry mixture through the sieve. Allow it to drip; don't press the mixture down, as this will make the liquid cloudy.

3 Heat ²/₃ cup (160ml) water in a small saucepan until simmering. Remove from the heat. Meanwhile, place the gelatine leaves in a bowl of cold water for 5 minutes. Squeeze out any excess water from the gelatine leaves, then add the gelatine to the pan of hot water. Stir to dissolve. Next, add the gelatine mixture to the strawberry liquid. Stir well to combine. Divide the unset jelly evenly among six 1¹/₄-cup (310ml) glasses. Refrigerate, covered, for at least 4 hours or overnight until set.

4 Put a metal tray in the freezer. Scoop out 6 small balls of the ice cream. Put the crushed meringue in a shallow bowl. Roll the ice cream balls in the meringue to coat. Place on the chilled metal tray. Cover with cling film. Freeze until needed.

5 To make the macerated strawberries, combine the ingredients in a bowl. Allow to stand for 10 minutes.

6 Spoon the macerated strawberries over the jellies. Top each one with a snowball. Sprinkle with the crushed pink peppercorns, if you like.

TIPS

- If you have the time, the strawberries used in step 1 can be left at a warm room temperature for 2 hours, instead of being heated.
- The strawberries remaining in the sieve at step 2 can be added to smoothies or drinks, or puréed to add to fruit sauces.
- The jellies can be made a day ahead.
- The snowballs can be prepared up to 4 hours in advance.
- The strawberries for the macerated strawberries can be sliced 4 hours ahead. Add sugar and juice 10 minutes before serving.

Lime and mango semifreddo

FROZEN | PREP + COOK TIME **20 MINUTES + STANDING + OVERNIGHT FREEZING** | SERVES **12**

As it is essentially a frozen mousse, semifreddo has a lighter texture than ice cream and is often more subtly flavoured as well. This makes it a refreshing end to a meal, particularly a substantial one, and this example with its tropical notes is no exception.

200ml extra thick double cream

1/2 cup (125ml) double cream

4 eggs, separated

1/3 cup (80ml) lime juice

1/2 cup (110g) caster sugar

2 small mangoes (600g), peeled, thinly sliced (see tips)

macadamia praline

1/4 cup (55g) caster sugar

1 cup (140g) unsalted macadamias, roasted, coarsely chopped

1/2 cup (25g) flaked coconut, toasted

TIPS

• You can use another seasonal fresh fruit instead of mango such as seasonal berries or figs, if you like. You can also use thawed frozen fruit.

• Instead of macadamias for the praline, try almonds or cashews.

• You will need to start this recipe at least 1 day ahead of serving. The semifreddo can be made up to 1 week ahead. Store, covered, in the freezer.

1 Lightly grease an 8cm x 33cm straight-sided loaf tin. Line with cling film, extending it 10cm over the long sides of the tin. Line a large baking tray with baking parchment.

2 To make the macadamia praline, heat the sugar in a medium frying pan over a medium-high heat for 2 minutes until bubbling and caramelized. Stir in the macadamias. Cook for a further 1 minute or until hot and well coated. Spread the nuts in a single layer on the lined tray. Set aside for 10 minutes or until cooled and firm.

3 Break the macadamia praline into large pieces. Reserve a quarter of the pieces to serve; store in an airtight container in a cool, dry place until needed. Process the remaining praline with the coconut until finely ground. Set aside.

4 Using an electric mixer, beat together both creams in a medium bowl until soft peaks form.

5 In a separate medium bowl, beat together the egg yolks, lime juice, and sugar with an electric mixer until pale and creamy.

6 Whisk the egg whites in a separate large bowl with an electric mixer until stiff peaks form.

7 Gently fold the egg yolk mixture into the cream mixture. Fold in the egg whites. Fold in the ground praline mixture until just combined; do not overmix. Spoon the mixture into the lined pan; smooth the surface. Fold the overhanging cling film over the mixture to cover. Freeze for 8 hours or overnight until firm.

8 To serve, stand the semifreddo at room temperature for 20 minutes before turning onto a platter. Decorate with the mango slices and reserved praline pieces.

Pomegranate and frozen yogurt cheesecakes

FROZEN | PREP + COOK TIME **40 MINUTES + FREEZING** | MAKES **4**

This recipe turns simple pre-purchased ingredients into an attractive and enticing dessert – and all with very little effort. Frozen yogurt adds tartness to the creamy filling, offset by fresh berries and tart-sweet pomegranate juice.

350g crunchy, sweet oat biscuits such as Hobnobs or ginger nut biscuits

70g butter, melted, plus extra for greasing

2 cups (300g) pomegranate seeds (see tips)

250g cream cheese, at room temperature

1/2 cup (110g) caster sugar

900ml carton vanilla Greek-style frozen yogurt

125g fresh blackberries

micro shiso, optional, to serve

1 Clip in the bases of six 10cm springform cake tins upside down, to form flat rather than recessed bases. Grease the tins. Line the bottoms and sides of the tins with baking parchment.

2 Put the biscuits in a zip-top bag. Using a rolling pin or meat mallet, crush the biscuits into coarse crumbs. Shake the crumbs in a coarse sieve to remove any fine crumbs; discard. Put the large crumbs in a medium bowl. Stir in the melted butter. Press about 1/3 cup of crumbs over the bottom of each prepared tin, pressing lightly to level. Freeze while preparing the filling.

3 Process 1 cup (150g) of the pomegranate seeds until finely chopped; reserve the rest for serving. Strain through a sieve over a jug to yield 1/2 cup (125ml) juice. Process the cream cheese and sugar using the pulse button until combined. Scrape down the side of the bowl. Add the pomegranate juice. Pulse until smooth. Add the frozen yogurt. Pulse until combined. Transfer to a large bowl. Freeze for 20 minutes or until firm but still able to be scooped.

4 Divide the mixture evenly among the cake tins. Smooth the tops. Cover tightly with cling film. Freeze for 4 hours or overnight until firm.

5 Remove the frozen cheesecakes from the cake tins. Decorate with the remaining pomegranate seeds, blackberries, and micro shiso, if using.

TIPS

- You will need about 2 large pomegranates for this recipe. Alternatively, purchase ready-prepared pomegranate seeds, available from greengrocers and supermarkets.
- To remove the seeds from a whole pomegranate, cut the pomegranate in half crossways. Hold it, cut-side down, in the palm of your hand over a bowl, then hit the outside firmly with a wooden spoon. The seeds should fall out easily; discard any white pith in the bowl. Scrape out any remaining seeds.
- Pomegranate seeds can be refrigerated in an airtight container for up to 4 days.
- The cheesecakes can be made to the end of step 4 up to a week ahead. Omit making the pomegranate juice and simply use 1/2 cup (125ml) purchased pomegranate juice instead.

Roasted pineapple with rum syrup

ROASTED | PREP + COOK TIME **1 HOUR 45 MINUTES** | SERVES **4**

Pineapple, rum, and lime form a classic trio of tropical flavours that will transport you straight to a tropical island in one bite! Serve with vanilla or butterscotch ice cream, if you like, and you will find it hard to let go of the culinary fantasy.

2 small pineapples (1.8kg)

6 whole star anise

150g caster sugar

1 cup (250ml) dark rum

100g unsalted butter, chopped

2 tbsp fresh mint leaves

2 limes (180g), cut into cheeks or wedges, to serve

1 Grease and line a large baking tray with baking parchment.

2 Peel and trim the pineapples. Reserve half of the trimmings. Halve the pineapples lengthways. Cut each half into 4 wedges. Cut out the core from each piece. Reserve the core pieces. Thread the pineapple pieces onto metal skewers. Pat the pineapple dry with kitchen paper.

3 Preheat a chargrill plate or barbecue to a high heat. Cook the pineapple skewers for 1 minute on each side or until grill marks appear. Transfer the pineapple to the lined tray; set aside.

4 Crush the star anise using a mortar and pestle (or use the base of a clean saucepan). Put in a medium heavy-based saucepan with the sugar, reserved pineapple cores and trimmings, and $1/4$ cup (60ml) water. Cook over a low heat, stirring, until the sugar has dissolved. Increase the heat to medium. Cook, without stirring, for 15 minutes or until a golden brown caramel forms, swirling the pan to colour evenly; the caramel will colour quickly once the process starts, so be careful not to overcook it.

5 Meanwhile, preheat the oven to 200°C (180°C fan/400°F/Gas 6).

6 Taking care, as the mixture will splutter, gradually add $3/4$ cup (185ml) of the rum to the caramel. Increase the heat to high. Boil for 2 minutes or until syrupy. Add the butter and 1 cup (250ml) water. Boil for 10 minutes until thick. Add the remaining $1/4$ cup (60ml) rum. Cook for a further 2 minutes. Strain into a heatproof jug. Discard the solids.

7 Brush the grilled pineapple with the rum syrup, reserving any leftover syrup. Roast the pineapple in the oven, basting every 10 minutes with the syrup, for 45 minutes or until tender and caramelized. Allow to cool slightly on the tray.

8 To serve, drizzle the pineapple skewers with the roasting juices and any remaining syrup. Sprinkle with the mint leaves, and serve with the lime cheeks for squeezing over.

TIPS

- Buy pineapples with the tops attached.
- Whole star anise are available from supermarkets. You can use cinnamon instead, if you like.
- Serve with vanilla or butterscotch ice cream.

Lemon sherbet granita

FROZEN | PREP + COOK TIME **10 MINUTES + COOLING + FREEZING** | SERVES **4**

Granitas do not usually contain dairy products, so this ice confection is more of a hybrid lying between a sherbet and a simple lemon granita – hence the name. With its zesty lemoniness, it possesses all the same palate-cleansing properties you'd expect and is just as easy to make.

1 cup (200g) caster sugar

2 lemons

$1/2$ cup (125ml) whipping cream

strips of lemon zest, to serve

1 Stir the sugar and $2^1/4$ cups (560ml) water in a medium saucepan over a low heat until the sugar dissolves.

2 Finely grate the zest of the lemons; you will need 1 tablespoon. Add the zest to the hot syrup. Allow to cool. Squeeze $1/2$ cup (125ml) lemon juice from the lemons. Add to the syrup with the cream; mix well to combine.

3 Pour into a 20cm x 30cm rectangular cake or brownie tin, or other shallow metal container.

4 Freeze for 2 hours. Use a fork to break up any ice crystals. Freeze for a further 9 hours, scraping with a fork every 3 hours or until frozen. Serve topped with strips of lemon zest.

Granita variations

Originally from Sicily, the granita is an integral element of Italy's love affair with frozen desserts – think gelato, sorbetto... the list goes on. Its name come from its grainy texture, which is achieved by forking through the flavoured syrup base during the freezing process.

Cucumber, mint, and lime granita

Stir $^3/_4$ cup (165g) caster sugar and $1^1/_2$ cups (375ml) water in a medium saucepan over a low heat until the sugar dissolves. Allow to cool. Process 3 midi or salad cucumbers (390g), $^1/_2$ cup (125ml) water, and 1 cup (20g) mint leaves until smooth. Strain through a fine sieve into a jug. Add the cooled syrup and $^1/_4$ cup (60ml) lime juice. Mix well. Pour into a 20cm x 30cm rectangular cake tin or shallow metal container. Freeze as instructed for the lemon sherbet granita on page 26.

Pineapple and strawberry granita

Stir $^3/_4$ cup (165g) caster sugar and $1^1/_2$ cups (375ml) water in a medium saucepan over a low heat until the sugar dissolves. Allow to cool. Process 250g trimmed fresh strawberries and 1 cup (250ml) pineapple juice until smooth. Add the strawberry mixture to a jug with the syrup and $^1/_4$ cup (60ml) lemon juice. Pour into a 20cm x 30cm rectangular cake tin or shallow metal container. Freeze as instructed for the lemon sherbet granita on page 26.

Nectarine and raspberry granita

Stir $^3/_4$ cup (165g) caster sugar and $1^1/_2$ cups (375ml) water in a medium saucepan over a low heat until the sugar dissolves. Allow to cool. Process 4 chopped ripe white nectarines (430g), 1 cup (125g) raspberries, and $^1/_4$ cup (60ml) lemon juice until smooth. Strain the nectarine mixture through a fine sieve into a jug with the syrup. Pour into a 20cm x 30cm rectangular cake tin or shallow metal container. Freeze as instructed for the lemon sherbet granita on page 26.

Passionfruit and elderflower granita

Stir $^3/_4$ cup (165g) caster sugar and $1^1/_2$ cups (375ml) water in a medium saucepan over a low heat until the sugar dissolves. Allow to cool. Combine the syrup with $1^1/_2$ cups (325ml) elderflower cordial, 1 cup (250ml) passionfruit pulp, and $^1/_4$ cup (60ml) freshly squeezed lemon juice in a large jug. Pour into a 20cm x 30cm rectangular cake tin or shallow metal container. Freeze as instructed for the lemon sherbet granita on page 26.

Apple, blackberry, and marzipan turnovers

BAKED | PREP + COOK TIME **40 MINUTES** | MAKES **4**

These individual pies are pleasure in an edible parcel, and the pairing of apples and blackberries is a classic one that is hard to beat. Use all-butter puff pastry for an extra decadent flavour and texture, and serve the pies topped with whipped cream, if you like.

1 green-skinned apple (150g)

2 tbsp granulated sugar

1 cup (150g) frozen blackberries

1 tsp cornflour

80g marzipan, finely chopped

2 sheets of frozen puff pastry

1   Preheat the oven to 180°C (160°C fan/350°F/Gas 4). Line 2 baking trays with baking parchment.

2   Peel and core the apple. Cut into 1cm pieces. Put the apple in a bowl with the blackberries, 1 tablespoon of the sugar, the cornflour, and marzipan. Stir well to combine, ensuring the fruit is evenly coated in both sugar and cornflour.

3   Cut the pastry sheets in half. Place one-quarter of the fruit mixture on one half of each pastry rectangle, leaving a border on all sides. Fold the opposite end over to enclose the fruit. Press the edges together with a fork to seal. Place the pies on the lined baking trays. Using a sharp knife, cut 3 slits across the top of each one. Brush lightly with a little water. Sprinkle with the remaining sugar.

4   Bake the pies for 25 minutes or until the pastry is puffed and golden. Serve warm.

TIPS

• You can use either Granny Smith or Golden Delicious apples. Granny Smith apples keep their shape, but Golden Delicious have a nicer flavour.

• Use other frozen berries instead of blackberries. Raspberries, mixed berries, and cherries would all work well here.

Plum and mascarpone tart

BAKED | PREP + COOK TIME **1 HOUR 40 MINUTES + REFRIGERATION** | SERVES **10**

Either moscato or a sweet rosé would work well in this recipe. The key to cooking with wine – which is used here to poach the plums – is never to cook with anything that you wouldn't actually enjoy drinking.

1 cup (150g) plain flour

$^1/_2$ cup (55g) hazelnut meal

$^1/_3$ cup (55g) icing sugar, plus extra 1 tbsp, sifted

125g chilled butter, chopped

1 egg yolk

1 tsp chilled water

$1^1/_2$ cups (375ml) dessert wine

$^3/_4$ cup (165g) caster sugar

1 vanilla pod, split lengthways

5 ripe plums (600g), quartered, stones removed

500g mascarpone

300ml double cream

1 tbsp almond-flavoured liqueur

TIPS

- Instead of using amaretto liqueur, you can substitute 1 teaspoon almond extract, if you like.
- If you put the pastry in the freezer instead of the fridge, you can reduce the resting time by half.
- The tart case can be made a day ahead. Store in an airtight container.
- The poached plums in step 2 can be made several hours ahead of time. Refrigerate, still in the syrup, in an airtight container.

1 Process the flour, hazelnut meal, and the $^1/_3$ cup (55g) icing sugar until just combined. Add the chilled butter; process again until the mixture resembles breadcrumbs. Add the combined yolk and 1 teaspoon chilled water; pulse until just combined. Form the dough into a disc, then wrap in cling film. Refrigerate for 1 hour.

2 Meanwhile, stir the wine, caster sugar, and vanilla pod in a deep medium frying pan over a medium heat until the sugar dissolves. Bring to the boil. Add the plums. Simmer for 3 minutes or until just tender. Allow the plums to cool, still in the syrup, in the pan.

3 Roll out the pastry between floured sheets of baking parchment until 4mm thick and large enough to line a 24cm loose-bottomed round fluted tart tin. Lift the pastry into the tin, easing it into the bottom and side. Trim the pastry edge. Cover. Refrigerate for 1 hour or until firm. (The pastry is quite delicate and may need to be chilled after rolling.)

4 Preheat the oven to 200°C (180°C fan/400°F/Gas 6). Place the tart tin on a baking tray. Line the pastry with baking parchment; fill with dried beans or rice. Bake blind for 20 minutes. Carefully remove the parchment and beans. Bake for a further 10 minutes or until golden and cooked through. Allow to cool.

5 Meanwhile, strain the plums, reserving the syrup and vanilla pod. Peel the plums. Return the reserved syrup to the pan. Simmer for 20 minutes until reduced by half. Allow to cool. Return the plums to the syrup.

6 Put the mascarpone, cream, liqueur, and extra 1 tablespoon sifted icing sugar in a large bowl. Using a wooden spoon, fold the ingredients until combined. Cover with cling film. Refrigerate.

7 Place the tart case on a serving platter. Spoon the mascarpone mixture into the tart case, then top with the poached plums and reserved vanilla pod. Drizzle with a little syrup. Serve immediately.

Apricot and verjuice pavlovas

BAKED | PREP + COOK TIME **2 HOURS + COOLING + REFRIGERATION** | MAKES **6**

Verjuice is a condiment made from the pressed juice of unripe grapes. It adds a wonderful acidity to sweet and savoury dishes without being too astringent. And that makes it ideal for complementing the crisp meringue of these mini pavlovas.

3 eggs, at room temperature

1¹/₂ cups (330g) caster sugar

1 bunch of fresh rosemary

2 cups (500ml) verjuice

1 cup (150g) dried apricot halves

40g butter, at room temperature

250g crème fraîche

1 Preheat the oven to 120°C (110°C fan/250°F/Gas ¹/₂). Line a large baking tray with baking parchment.

2 Separate the eggs, putting the whites in the bowl of an electric mixer and the yolks in a small cup. Reserve the yolks. Using the electric mixer, beat the egg whites until soft peaks form. With the motor operating, gradually add ³/₄ cup (165g) of the caster sugar, beating until the sugar dissolves and the mixture is thick and glossy. Dollop 6 large spoonfuls of the meringue onto the lined baking tray.

3 Bake the pavlovas for 1¹/₂ hours or until firm and dry. Turn off the oven Allow the pavlovas to cool in the oven with the door ajar. When completely cold, store in an airtight container until ready to serve.

4 Meanwhile, combine the remaining ³/₄ cup (165g) sugar, ²/₃ cup (160ml) water, 2 sprigs of rosemary, and the verjuice in a medium saucepan over a medium heat. Bring to the boil, stirring to dissolve the sugar. Cook for 2 minutes. Add the dried apricots; return to the boil. Cook for 3 minutes or until tender. Allow to cool.

5 To make the apricot curd, in a small saucepan, whisk together the reserved egg yolks and 1 cup (250ml) of the apricot poaching liquid. Cook, stirring continuously, over a low heat for 4 minutes or until well thickened (do not allow to boil). Remove the pan from the heat. Whisk in the butter. Strain the curd into a small bowl. Cover the surface directly with cling film. Refrigerate for 3 hours or until set.

6 Serve the pavlovas topped with the crème fraîche, apricot curd, and poached apricots in the remaining syrup.

TIPS

- Make the pavlovas and the poached apricots up to a day ahead. Store the pavlovas in an airtight container at room temperature and the apricots in the fridge.
- For a flavourful alternative, add ¹/₂ teaspoon ground cardamom to the whipped egg whites with the sugar in step 2. Alternatively, add strips of orange zest to the syrup in step 4.
- To make a festive garnish from the remaining rosemary sprigs, brush them with an extra egg white, then sprinkle with 1 tablespoon caster sugar. Place on a separate baking tray, and bake for 1 hour alongside the pavlovas until dried.

Fig and vincotto bread pudding

BAKED | PREP + COOK TIME **1 HOUR 20 MINUTES + STANDING** | SERVES **6**

Vincotto is produced in several regions of Italy, with some areas such as Puglia having their own specific variations. The vincotto of Marche and Abruzzo, known as vino cotto, is actually a wine. Vincotto is commonly used as a condiment in both sweet and savoury cooking.

100g (3oz) butter

500g sourdough fruit and walnut loaf

6 eggs

1/2 cup (110g) caster sugar

1 litre (4 cups) milk

6 large fresh figs (480g) (see tips)

1/2 cup (125ml) fig or other vincotto (see tips)

1 Using some of the butter, grease a 23cm round, 6cm deep (2-litre/8-cup) ovenproof dish.

2 Remove the crusts from the bread. Cut the bread into 5mm thick slices. Spread the slices with the remaining butter. Arrange the bread slices in a circular pattern in the dish. Whisk together the eggs, sugar, and milk in a large jug until combined. Pour over the bread. Allow to stand for 30 minutes for the bread to soften.

3 Meanwhile, preheat the oven to 180°C (160°C fan/350°F/Gas 4).

4 Place the pudding dish in a large roasting pan. Add enough boiling water to the pan to come halfway up the side of the dish. Gently transfer the pan to the oven. Bake the pudding for 50 minutes or until just set.

5 Cut the figs into slices or wedges. Serve the pudding topped with the figs and drizzled with the vincotto.

TIPS

- You can use green or black figs, but for the best flavour they must be ripe.
- Vincotto translates from Italian as 'cooked wine'. Traditionally it is made by boiling down grape must – the juice and pulp of wine-making grapes – to make a thick, versatile syrupy condiment. It is available from Italian delis and speciality grocers.
- If you can't find vincotto, you can use balsamic glaze or reduced balsamic vinegar instead.
- If you like, add 1 teaspoon ground cinnamon to the butter before spreading on the bread for something a little different.

Black Forest soufflé

BAKED | PREP + COOK TIME **55 MINUTES** | SERVES **4**

Two classic desserts combine scrumptiously and effortlessly in this easy recipe, where
a light-as-air French soufflé meets the kirsch-spiked cherry and chocolate flavours of
Germany's Black Forest gateau.

60g butter, melted

2 tbsp caster sugar, plus extra $1/3$ cup (75g)

300g dark chocolate (at least 70% cocoa)

6 eggs, at room temperature, separated

3 egg whites, at room temperature

2 tsp icing sugar

double cream, to serve

poached cherries

415g canned seedless black cherries in syrup

$1/4$ cup (55g) caster sugar

5cm strip of orange zest

2 tbsp kirsch or cherry brandy

1. To make the poached cherries, drain the cherries over a bowl. Reserve the syrup and cherries separately. Stir together the syrup, caster sugar, and orange zest in a medium saucepan. Next, stir over a high heat, without boiling, until the sugar dissolves. Bring to the boil. Reduce the heat. Simmer, uncovered, for about 5 minutes or until the syrup thickens slightly. Remove from the heat. Stir in the cherries and kirsch.

2. Preheat the oven to 200°C (180°C fan/400°F/Gas 6). Grease four $1^1/4$-cup (310ml) ovenproof soufflé dishes with the melted butter; sprinkle the butter with the 2 tablespoons caster sugar. Shake out any excess sugar.

3. Break the chocolate into a large heatproof bowl over a large saucepan of simmering water (don't let the water touch the base of the bowl). Stir until the chocolate is melted. Allow to cool for 5 minutes. Stir in the egg yolks until smooth and combined.

4. Using an electric mixer, beat all 9 egg whites and the extra $1/3$ cup (75g) sugar in a medium bowl until soft peaks form. Working in 2 batches, gently fold into the chocolate mixture. Divide the mixture among the prepared soufflé dishes. Smooth the tops. Carefully place the dishes on a baking tray. Bake the soufflés for about 15 minutes until puffed and risen.

5. Dust the soufflés with the sifted icing sugar. Serve immediately with the poached cherries and a dollop of double cream.

TIP

Serve with vanilla bean ice cream instead of
the double cream or, for a real treat, use both!

Lemon passionfruit creams with shortbread

BAKED AND SET | PREP + COOK TIME **45 MINUTES + OVERNIGHT REFRIGERATION** | SERVES **6**

Buttery shortbread provides a foil for these unctuous syllabub-like desserts. While fresh passionfruit pulp is best for this recipe, if you can't find fresh passionfruit, you can use canned pulp instead. Just ensure there isn't any added sugar.

You will need to start this recipe a day ahead

3 large lemons (600g)

600ml double cream

$^1/_4$ cup (55g) caster sugar,
plus extra $^1/_3$ cup (75g)

$^1/_3$ cup (80g) passionfruit pulp

175g cold butter

$1^2/_3$ cups (250g) plain flour

150g fresh blueberries

1 Finely grate the zest from the lemons; you will need 1 tablespoon lemon zest. Squeeze the juice from 1½ of the lemons; you will need ¼ cup (60ml) lemon juice.

2 Put the cream and $^1/_4$ cup (55g) caster sugar in a heavy-based saucepan over a high heat. Stir continuously until the mixture boils. Reduce the heat to medium. Simmer, stirring, for a further 2 minutes. Remove from the heat. Allow to cool for 10 minutes.

3 Add the $^1/_4$ cup (60ml) lemon juice and 2 teaspoons of the zest to the cream mixture. Stir gently for 5 seconds. Do not overmix. Pour into six $^3/_4$-cup (180ml) glasses or small wide bowls. Spoon half of the passionfruit pulp into the lemon mixture. Refrigerate overnight until set.

4 To make the lemon shortbread, chop the cold butter. Process the flour, the extra $^1/_3$ cup (75g) sugar, remaining lemon zest, and chopped butter until combined. With the motor operating, add 1 tablespoon cold water. Process until the mixture forms a soft ball. Divide the dough in half. Flatten each portion into a disc. Wrap each one in cling film. Refrigerate for 20 minutes or until firm.

5 Preheat the oven to 180°C (160°C fan/350°F/Gas 4).

6 Roll out each disc of shortbread between lightly floured sheets of baking parchment until 3mm thick. Remove the top sheet of baking parchment; transfer the dough on the paper to the baking trays. Bake for 15 minutes or until the shortbread is golden. Cut into shards while still warm. Allow to cool on the trays.

7 Top the lemon passionfruit creams with the remaining passionfruit and the blueberries. Serve with the lemon shortbread.

TIPS

• The citric acid in the lemon reacts with the cream to thicken it.
• Top with sliced strawberries or torn raspberries instead of blueberries, if you like.
• The shortbread can be stored in an airtight container for up to 1 week.

Frozen raspberry, yogurt, and strawberry terrine

FROZEN | PREP + COOK TIME **1 HOUR + FREEZING, REFRIGERATION + STANDING** | SERVES **10**

This dessert is a celebration of berries. Be sure to make it when berries are at their peak season for the best flavour. The smooth-textured fruit sorbets are 'churned' using a food processor, then layered with yogurt sorbet to make the very berry terrine.

250g raspberries

250g strawberries, hulled, quartered

1/4 cup (55g) caster sugar

1/3 cup (15g) firmly packed small mint leaves

raspberry sorbet

250g frozen raspberries

1/4 cup (60ml) boiling water

1 tbsp glucose syrup

2 tbsp pure icing sugar

yogurt sorbet

1/2 cup (125ml) milk

1/4 cup (55g) caster sugar

1 tbsp glucose syrup

3/4 cup (200g) Greek-style yogurt

strawberry sorbet

250g strawberries, halved

1/4 cup (60ml) boiling water

1 tbsp glucose syrup

1/4 cup (55g) pure icing sugar

1 Line the bottom and sides of a 7cm x 20cm top measurement, 9cm x 22cm base measurement, 1 litre (4-cup) loaf tin with cling film. Freeze until needed.

2 Make the raspberry sorbet. Process the raspberries until coarsely crushed. Combine the water and glucose in a small jug. Gradually add to the processor while the motor is operating. Process for 3 minutes or until smooth. Add the icing sugar. Process until combined. Spoon the mixture into the prepared loaf tin. Smooth the surface. Cover with foil, then freeze for 2 hours or until firm.

3 Make the yogurt sorbet. Stir the milk, caster sugar, and glucose in a small saucepan until the sugar is dissolved. Bring to the boil. Remove from the heat. Allow to cool, then whisk in the yogurt. Refrigerate until cold. Remove the foil from the raspberry sorbet, and spoon the cold yogurt sorbet over the top of it. Smooth the surface. Cover again with foil. Freeze for 4 hours or until firm.

4 Make the strawberry sorbet. Process the strawberries until coarsely chopped. Combine the water and glucose in a small jug. Gradually add to the processor while the motor is operating. Process for 3 minutes or until smooth. Add the icing sugar. Process until combined. Refrigerate until cold. Remove the foil from the tin, and spoon the cold strawberry sorbet over the yogurt sorbet. Smooth the surface. Cover once more with foil. Leave to freeze overnight.

5 Combine the raspberries, strawberries, caster sugar, and half of the mint leaves in a medium bowl. Allow to stand at room temperature for 20 minutes, stirring occasionally, or until the sugar is dissolved.

6 Turn the terrine out of the loaf tin. Serve topped with the berry mixture and remaining mint leaves.

Cookie dough and blackberry ice cream loaf

FROZEN | PREP + COOK TIME **15 MINUTES + FREEZING + STANDING** | SERVES **8**

The longest part of making this dessert is the freezing time, yet it looks as if you have slaved over it for hours. To make a bespoke dessert, use your favourite ice cream flavour in place of the vanilla. Chocolate and caramel-flavoured ice cream would work very well in this recipe.

1 litre (4 cups) good-quality vanilla bean ice cream

$^2/_3$ cup (100g) roasted salted macadamias, plus extra, to serve (optional)

200g purchased edible chocolate chip cookie dough (see tips)

$^1/_2$ cup (125ml) purchased chocolate topping or chocolate syrup, plus extra, to serve (optional)

$^1/_2$ cup (75g) fresh or frozen blackberries, plus extra, to serve (optional)

1 Scoop half of the ice cream into a medium bowl (return the remaining half to the freezer until needed). Allow to stand for 15 minutes or until softened slightly.

2 Grease a 13.5cm x 24cm (9-cup capacity) loaf tin. Line the bottom and long sides with baking parchment, extending the paper 2cm over the sides. Sprinkle the macadamias over the bottom of the tin.

3 Chop the cookie dough into 1cm pieces. Add the cookie dough to the softened ice cream with $^1/_4$ cup (60ml) of the chocolate topping. Stir through until smooth. Spread the ice cream mixture over the macadamias. Spread the remaining chocolate topping over the ice cream mixture. Freeze for 1 hour or until firm.

4 After 45 minutes, remove the remaining vanilla ice cream from the freezer. Scoop into a medium bowl to soften. Stir through the $^1/_2$ cup (75g) blackberries. Spread the blackberry ice cream mixture over the cookie dough ice cream in the loaf tin. Freeze for 4 hours or overnight until firm.

5 Remove the ice cream loaf from the freezer 10 minutes before serving, to allow it to soften slightly. Serve in thick slices with extra macadamias, blackberries, and chocolate topping, if you like.

TIPS

• It is not advisable to eat home-made raw cookie dough. Purpose-made frozen edible cookie dough uses pasteurized eggs and heat-treated flour, to ensure food safety. If you cannot find it, simply use cookie dough ice cream instead, halving the amount of vanilla bean ice cream and using it only for the blackberry half of the ice cream loaf.

• If you don't have a loaf tin exactly the dimensions specified in the recipe that is OK, as long as the cup capacity is similar. To check the cup capacity of your dish, fill it to the rim with cup measures of water, keeping track of how much you add.

• You can make the ice cream loaf up to 3 days ahead. Cover and freeze until needed.

• Use other frozen berries such as raspberries or strawberries, instead of the blackberries, or when fresh berries are not in season.

Mango cheesecake tart

BAKED AND FRESH | PREP + COOK TIME **1 HOUR 5 MINUTES + REFRIGERATION** | SERVES **6**

The shape and size of this crowd-pleasing dessert make it easy to cut and serve to a larger gathering of guests, and its straightforward final assembly means that you won't be stuck in the kitchen while everyone else is enjoying themselves.

1½ cups (225g) plain flour

2 tbsp caster sugar, plus extra ¼ cup (55g)

75g butter

500g cream cheese, softened

¼ cup (20g) moist coconut flakes

⅓ cup (80ml) milk

2 mangoes (860g)

1 To make the pastry base, process the flour, the 2 tablespoons caster sugar, butter, and 125g of the cream cheese until a dough starts to form. Knead the dough on a lightly floured work surface until just combined. Wrap in cling film. Refrigerate for 30 minutes.

2 Roll the pastry between 2 lightly floured sheets of baking parchment until large enough to line an 11cm x 35cm loose-bottomed rectangular tart tin. Lift the pastry into the tin, easing into the bottom and sides. Trim the edges. Prick the bottom of the pastry case with a fork. Refrigerate for 10 minutes.

3 Meanwhile, put the coconut flakes on a baking tray. Place in the cold oven, then turn to 180°C (160°C fan/350°F/Gas 4) to preheat for the tart. Roast the coconut for 6 minutes or until lightly golden. Set aside.

4 Line the pastry case with baking parchment. Fill with dried beans or rice. Bake blind for 15 minutes. Remove the parchment and beans. Bake for a further 20 minutes or until the pastry is golden. Allow to cool.

5 Meanwhile, process the milk, the extra ¼ cup (55g) caster sugar, and the remaining cream cheese until smooth. Spoon the mixture into the cooled tart case, spreading evenly over the bottom.

6 Cut cheeks from the mangoes. Using a large metal spoon, scoop to remove the cheek flesh from the skin in one piece. Cut lengthways into thin slices. Arrange the mango slices on top of the tart. Serve the tart scattered with the toasted coconut.

TIPS

• Cut the flesh from around the mango stone and freeze for use in smoothies.

• Add 2 teaspoons vanilla bean paste or finely grated lime zest to the filling mixture, if you like.

• You can use yellow-fleshed pineapple or star fruit instead of the mango for an equally tropical feel.

Mixed berry clafoutis

BAKED | PREP + COOK TIME **45 MINUTES** | SERVES **4**

The classic dessert clafoutis, from the Limousin region of France, traditionally consists of black cherries baked in a sweet, custard-like batter. Here, we've swapped the cherries for mixed berries such as strawberries and blackberries, for a flavourful twist.

a little softened butter, for greasing

²/₃ cup (160ml) milk

²/₃ cup (160ml) double cream

1 cinnamon stick

1 tsp vanilla extract

4 eggs

¹/₂ cup (110g) caster sugar

¹/₄ cup (35g) plain flour

2 cups (300g) frozen mixed berries

icing sugar, sifted, for dusting

vanilla ice cream or whipped cream, to serve (optional)

1 Preheat the oven to 200°C (180°C fan/400°F/Gas 6). Grease a 1.5-litre (6-cup) ovenproof dish.

2 Put the milk, cream, cinnamon, and vanilla extract in a medium saucepan. Bring to the boil, then immediately remove from the heat. Discard the cinnamon stick.

3 Whisk together the eggs and sugar in a medium bowl until light and frothy. Whisk in the flour, then gradually whisk in the milk-cream mixture.

4 Sprinkle the berries over the bottom of the prepared dish. Pour the batter over the berries. Bake for 35 minutes or until lightly browned and set. Serve the clafoutis warm, dusted with sifted icing sugar and topped with a scoop of ice cream, if you like.

Elderflower, vodka, and cranberry ice pops

FROZEN | PREP + COOK TIME **25 MINUTES + FREEZING** | MAKES **24**

Ice lollies for adults, these are wonderful served at parties and gatherings during the long days of summer. Tart and fresh, with floral and minty undertones, once served these treats will not last long enough even to begin to melt.

¹/₃ cup (80ml) vodka

¹/₂ cup (125ml) elderflower cordial

2 tbsp strained lime juice

1 cup (250ml) sparkling mineral water

2 tbsp thinly sliced mint leaves

3 cups (750ml) cranberry juice

1 Combine the vodka, elderflower cordial, lime juice, and mineral water in a medium jug. Divide the mixture evenly among the ice lolly moulds (see tips). Sprinkle evenly with the mint. Wrap the mould completely in cling film. Insert the ice lolly sticks into the holes, piercing the cling film (the cling film will help to keep the sticks upright while the ice pops set). Freeze for 6 hours or until the mixture is frozen.

2 Pour the cranberry juice over the vodka mint layer. Freeze for 2 hours or until the juice is frozen.

3 Just before serving, rub the outside of the moulds with a hot kitchen cloth to loosen. Gently remove the ice pops, and serve immediately.

TIPS

- You will need 24 x ¹/₄-cup (60ml) ice lolly moulds and 24 ice lolly sticks.
- We used 60ml shot glasses and lollipop sticks to make our ice pops. You could also use small plastic cups. Follow the same instructions as in step 1 for covering with cling film, then piercing with the lollipop sticks, to make sure the sticks remain in place while the ice pops set.
- The ice pops can be made several days ahead.

CHOCOLATE AND COFFEE

Rich mousses, spectacular tarts and pastries,
puddings and soufflés oozy with goodness –
this is the place for those of us for whom
chocolate and coffee are flavour imperatives.

Coffee and crunch ice cream wreath

FROZEN | PREP + COOK TIME **45 MINUTES + FREEZING** | SERVES **12**

Serving this frozen dessert in the form of a wreath gives it a celebratory feel – and makes it easy to serve in slices where everyone gets to enjoy a little of the goodies sprinkled on top. The coffee-macadamia ice cream sits on a malty chocolate base, adding to the enticement.

You will need to start this recipe a day ahead

butter for greasing

2 tbsp instant coffee granules

1½ tbsp coffee liqueur

600ml double cream

2½ cups (400g) pure icing sugar, sifted

500g mascarpone

¼ cup (45g) chocolate-coated coffee beans, chopped, plus extra, to serve

1 cup (140g) coarsely chopped honey-roasted macadamias

30 purchased chocolates, such as truffles, chocolate stars, and chocolate-coated malt balls, to decorate (see tips)

cocoa powder, sifted, to dust (optional)

biscuit base

250g chocolate chip biscuits

1 cup (100g) chocolate-coated malt balls

60g butter, melted

TIPS

- Choose a mix of white, milk, and dark chocolate, in varying sizes and shapes, for the best visual effect.
- Be careful not to overmix the recipe in step 3, as this will cause a grainy texture and mouthfeel in the finished dessert.
- The wreath can be made up to 3 days ahead.

1 Grease a 24cm springform cake tin. Line the bottom and side with baking parchment. Wrap a 9cm round ramekin (or other straight-sided round dish) with a double layer of cling film. Grease the plastic. Place in the centre of the tin.

2 Combine the coffee granules and ¼ cup (60ml) boiling water in a small jug. Stir to dissolve, then stir in the liqueur. Allow to cool.

3 Using an electric mixer, beat together the cream and icing sugar in a large bowl until soft peaks form. Fold in the mascarpone, the ¼ cup (45g) chocolate-coated coffee beans, and ¾ cup (105g) of the macadamias, then fold in the coffee mixture until just combined.

4 Spoon the mixture into the prepared tin. Smooth the top. Freeze for 4 hours or until firm.

5 Meanwhile, to make the biscuit base, process the biscuits and malt balls into coarse crumbs. Add the melted butter. Process briefly to combine.

6 Press the biscuit mixture over the top of the ice cream to form a smooth surface. Freeze overnight.

7 To serve, remove the ramekin in the middle of the tin, and release the side from the tin (if needed, rub the outside of the cake tin with a hot damp cloth). Place an inverted serving plate on top of the biscuit base and carefully turn over. Remove the bottom of the pan and the baking parchment. Top the ice cream wreath with the remaining macadamias, chocolates, and extra chocolate-coated coffee beans. Dust with a little sifted cocoa powder, if you like.

Figgy brownies with chocolate butterscotch sauce

BAKED | PREP + COOK TIME **45 MINUTES** | MAKES **9**

Ice cream performs double duty in this recipe, acting as a unique trick to create a decadent dessert sauce as well as an accompaniment to the brownies. Soft, moist figs add a rich sweetness to the brownies, completing the symphony of culinary gratification.

250g soft dried figs (see tip)

400g dark chocolate (70% cocoa)

125g unsalted butter, plus extra for greasing

3/4 cup (165g) caster sugar

3 eggs

2/3 cup (100g) self-raising flour

3 cups (750ml) butterscotch ice cream

1 Preheat the oven to 180°C (160°C fan/350°F/Gas 4). Lightly grease a 20cm square cake tin. Line the bottom with baking parchment.

2 Remove and discard the hard tops from the figs. Coarsely chop the figs. Break the chocolate into squares. Cut the butter into cubes.

3 Place 200g of the chocolate, the butter, and caster sugar in a large heatproof bowl over a large saucepan of simmering water (don't allow the base of the bowl to touch the water). Stir until melted. Allow to cool. Reserve the pan of water.

4 Whisk the eggs into the chocolate mixture until combined. Next, fold through the flour and salt until just combined. Fold in the figs until just combined. Pour the brownie mixture into the prepared cake tin.

5 Bake for 25 minutes or until a wooden skewer inserted into the centre comes out with moist crumbs attached. Leave in the tin for 5 minutes.

6 Meanwhile, to make the chocolate butterscotch sauce, reheat the reserved pan of water over a low-medium heat until simmering. Place 150g of the remaining chocolate in a large heatproof bowl with 1 cup (250ml) of the ice cream. Place the bowl over the pan of simmering water, then stir until melted and smooth. Remove the bowl from the pan. Finely grate the remaining chocolate.

7 Cut the brownie into 9 squares. Serve drizzled with the chocolate butterscotch sauce and sprinkled with the grated chocolate, accompanied by the remaining ice cream.

TIPS

- Soft, juicy figs are simply dried figs that are not as hard as traditional dried figs.
- Serve the brownies topped with toasted walnuts, almonds, or hazelnuts, if you like.
- Use good-quality vanilla or chocolate ice cream instead of butterscotch ice cream.

Cherry and orange chocolate puff

BAKED | PREP + COOK TIME **35 MINUTES + STANDING** | SERVES **6**

No one need ever know how simple it is to make this rich pastry. Using good-quality
block chocolate assures a result as smooth as the finest home-made chocolate sauce.
And chocolate and cherries are, it almost goes without saying, a divine combination.

2 sheets of frozen puff pastry, just thawed

200g block white chocolate

100g block thin orange-flavoured dark chocolate
(see tips)

2 tbsp dried cherries (see tips)

1 egg, lightly beaten

2 tbsp natural flaked almonds

2 tsp icing sugar, sifted

vanilla ice cream, to serve

1 Preheat the oven to 190°C (170°C fan/375°F/Gas 5). Line a baking tray
   with baking parchment.

2 Place 1 sheet of the puff pastry on the lined tray. Place the white
   chocolate block in the centre of the pastry. Top with the dark chocolate
   block. Cover the surface of the dark chocolate with the dried cherries.

3 Lightly brush the edges of the pastry with the beaten egg. Place the
   remaining pastry sheet over the top to cover the base. Trim 2cm from
   the sides of the pastry.

4 Gently fold the edges in a pleated pattern, from the outside inwards,
   around the chocolate. Tuck the ends upwards to seal. Lightly brush the
   pastry with more of the beaten egg. Scatter the almonds over the top.

5 Bake for 25 minutes or until the pastry is cooked through and golden.
   Allow to stand on the tray for 15 minutes.

6 Dust the puff with the sifted icing sugar. Serve in slices, accompanied
   by the vanilla ice cream.

TIPS

- Use your favourite type and flavour of chocolate,
if you like. Try raspberry for a nice substitute
- You can also swap the dried cherries for dried
cranberries, sultanas, raisins, or chopped nuts,
- The puff can be made a day ahead to the end of
step 4. Bake just before serving.
- If you like to make your own puff pastry instead of
using frozen, try using chocolate puff pastry instead
of plain, for an extra special dessert.

Chocolate tartlets with berries

BAKED | PREP + COOK TIME **40 MINUTES + COOLING** | MAKES **6**

Rich chocolate and tart–sweet berries are a match made in heaven. Using puff pastry instead of a traditional sweet shortcrust for these tartlets not only is quicker, but lightens this decadent flavour pairing as well.

butter for greasing

3 egg yolks

1/2 cup (110g) caster sugar

2 tbsp cornflour

1 tbsp cocoa powder

3/4 cup (180ml) milk

2/3 cup (160ml) double cream

1 sheet of puff pastry, just thawed

150g fresh raspberries

150g fresh blueberries

1 tbsp icing sugar, sifted

1 Preheat the oven to 220°C (200°C fan/425°F/Gas 7). Grease six holes of a 12-hole (1/3-cup/80ml) muffin tin.

2 To make the chocolate custard filling, combine the egg yolks, caster sugar, cornflour, and cocoa powder in a medium saucepan. Whisk in the milk and cream until smooth. Stir over a medium heat until the mixture boils and thickens. Transfer to a heatproof bowl; cover the surface with cling film. Allow to cool.

3 Meanwhile, cut the pastry sheet in half. Stack the 2 halves; press firmly. Roll up the pastry tightly from the short side. Cut the log into 6 slices, then roll the slices between sheets of baking parchment into 12cm rounds. Press the rounds into the holes of the prepared muffin tin.

4 Pour the chocolate custard into the pastry cases. Bake for about 20 minutes or until set. Allow to cool in the tin.

5 Serve the tarts topped with the raspberries and blueberries, then dusted with the sifted icing sugar.

Profiteroles

BAKED | PREP + COOK TIME **1 HOUR 10 MINUTES + COOLING** | MAKES **16**

These pastries become profiteroles when they're filled, but are not your commonly seen version filled with whipped cream and topped with chocolate sauce. Instead, classic choux pastry sandwiches a scoop of ice cream and is simply dusted with a little icing sugar.

60g butter, chopped

1 tsp caster sugar

³/₄ cup (110g) plain flour

3 eggs

1.5 litres (6 cups) vanilla ice cream, softened slightly

icing sugar, sifted, to dust

1　Preheat the oven to 200°C (180°C fan/400°F/Gas 6). Lightly grease 2 baking trays.

2　Combine ³/₄ cup (180ml) water, the butter, and the sugar in a medium saucepan over a low heat until the butter has melted. Bring to the boil. Add the flour. Beat with a wooden spoon for 2 minutes or until the mixture comes away from the bottom of the pan.

3　Transfer the pastry to the small bowl of an electric mixer. Beat in the eggs one at a time, beating well after each addition, until the dough is smooth and glossy.

4　Drop 16 level tablespoons of the dough onto the prepared trays, placing them 5cm apart. Bake for 20 minutes. Reduce the oven temperature to 180°C (160°C fan/350°F/Gas 4). Bake for a further 10 minutes or until golden and firm. Turn off the oven, and allow the profiteroles to cool in the oven with the door ajar.

5　Using a sharp knife, split the profiteroles in half. Fill each one with a scoop of ice cream. Dust the profiteroles with a little icing sugar.

TIP

Use your favourite flavour of ice cream such as chocolate, salted caramel, or honeycomb instead of vanilla. Or try the coffee and caramel variation on page 64. You will find a cream-filled option topped with chocolate there, too.

Profiteroles variations

You don't need to be daunted at the idea of making your own profiteroles. Tackling choux pastry is not difficult as long as you follow the instructions with care, and you can then mix it up with the fillings by using any of the combinations below.

Cream filling and chocolate sauce

Make the profiteroles as described through to the end of step 4 on page 62. To make the chocolate sauce, chop 100g each of dark and milk chocolate. Place in a small saucepan with $1/2$ cup double cream. Stir over a low heat until just smooth. For the filling, whisk 1 cup (250g) mascarpone, 1 cup (250ml) double cream, 1 teaspoon vanilla extract, and 2 teaspoons icing sugar to soft peaks. Fill the split profiteroles with the mascarpone cream. Drizzle with the chocolate sauce.

Custard and toffee

Make the profiteroles as described through to the end of step 4 on page 62. Beat 1 cup (250g) mascarpone with $1/2$ cup (125ml) ready-made dairy custard until thick. Fill the split profiteroles with the custard. Place on a foil-covered tray. Stir 1 cup (220g) caster sugar and $1/2$ cup (125ml) water in a saucepan over a medium heat, without boiling, until dissolved. Boil without stirring until golden; be careful not to burn, and bear in mind that the toffee will continue to darken after being removed from the heat. Drizzle the profiteroles with the toffee. (Take care, as it will be very hot.)

Crushed berries and cream

Make the profiteroles as described through to the end of step 4 on page 62. Combine 150g raspberries and 2 tablespoons icing sugar in a bowl. Mash with a fork until soft. Add 1.5 litres (6 cups) softened vanilla ice cream. Fold together. Fill each of the split profiteroles with a scoop of the raspberry ice cream. Freeze. Stir $1/2$ cup (160g) berry jam and $1/2$ cup (125ml) pomegranate juice in a saucepan over a medium heat for 3 minutes or until thickened. Serve the profiteroles drizzled with the syrup.

Coffee ice cream and caramel

Make the profiteroles as on page 62 using coffee or caramel ice cream instead of vanilla and folding in $1^1/2$ cups (225g) chopped Vienna or caramelized almonds. Freeze. Stir 380g canned Carnation Caramel filling or dulce de leche in a small saucepan over a medium heat with 2 tablespoons each of rum and water until smooth and a drizzling consistency. Serve the profiteroles drizzled with the warm rum-caramel sauce.

Chocolate soufflé with chocolate and sherry sauce

BAKED | PREP + COOK TIME 45 MINUTES + COOLING | MAKES 8

The best sweet sherry to use in this recipe is Pedro Ximénez. A dark, syrupy style of sherry, it has a wonderful affinity with chocolate. Whichever particular sherry you choose, it should always be good-quality and something that you would happily drink.

50g butter, softened

$^1/_3$ cup (75g) caster sugar

6 eggs

$1^1/_4$ cups (310ml) milk

275g dark chocolate (70% cocoa), broken into squares

1 tbsp cornflour

$^1/_4$ cup (60ml) sweet sherry such as Pedro Ximénez (see tips)

TIPS

• For a flavour twist, use coffee- or orange-flavoured liqueur instead of the sherry.

• Keep the unused egg yolks, covered, in the fridge, to make your own mayonnaise, lemon butter, or hollandaise sauce.

• Serve with scoops of vanilla bean ice cream.

• You could also serve a small glass of sherry with the soufflés, if you like.

1 Preheat the oven to 190°C (170°C fan/375°F/Gas 5). Grease eight $^1/_2$-cup (125ml) ramekins or ovenproof dishes with soft butter. Coat the bottoms and sides with 2 tablespoons of the caster sugar, then shake out any excess. Place the ramekins on a baking tray.

2 Separate the eggs: place 6 egg whites in the bowl of an electric mixer and 3 egg yolks in a medium bowl. Keep the remaining egg yolks for another use (see tips).

3 Put 1 cup (250ml) of the milk in a medium saucepan over a medium heat. Add 100g of the chocolate squares to the pan. Stir with a whisk until the chocolate melts and the mixture is smooth and almost boiling.

4 Add the cornflour and remaining caster sugar to the egg yolks. Whisk until smooth. Whisk $^1/_4$ cup (60ml) of the hot chocolate mixture into the egg yolk mixture until combined. Pour the mixture back into the saucepan. Whisk continuously over a medium heat until the mixture boils and thickens. Transfer to a large bowl. Cover the surface directly with cling film. Allow to cool for 15 minutes.

5 Using an electric mixer, beat the egg whites until stiff peaks form. With a large metal spoon, stir one-third of the egg whites through the warm chocolate mixture. Fold in the remaining egg whites until just combined.

6 Spoon the soufflé mixture into the prepared ramekins. Smooth the surface level with the top of the dish. Run a small knife around the inside of each dish. Bake for 12 minutes or until the soufflés are puffed.

7 Meanwhile, to make the chocolate sauce, put the remaining chocolate in a small heavy-based saucepan. Add the remaining $^1/_4$ cup (60ml) milk and the sherry. Stir over a medium heat until smooth.

8 Serve the soufflés immediately, drizzled with the hot chocolate sauce.

Chocolate mousse shots

SET | PREP + COOK TIME **25 MINUTES + REFRIGERATION** | SERVES **4**

These chocolate 'shots' are the perfect size when you're craving something a little sweet, but possess the necessary restraint not to go overboard. The tart raspberries cut through the sweetness of the mousse beautifully. Sometimes less definitely is more.

50g dark chocolate (at least 70% cocoa), finely chopped

$1/2$ cup (120g) fresh soft ricotta at room temperature

$1/4$ cup (55g) caster sugar

3 tsp Dutch-process cocoa powder (see tips)

2 egg whites

125g fresh raspberries

1 Stir the chocolate in a medium heatproof bowl over a medium saucepan of simmering water (don't let the water touch the base of the bowl) until melted. Allow to cool for 10 minutes.

2 Meanwhile, process the ricotta with the caster sugar and cocoa powder until smooth. Add the melted chocolate. Process until combined.

3 Using an electric mixer, beat the egg whites in a small bowl until soft peaks form. Fold the egg whites into the chocolate mixture in 2 batches. Pour the mixture into four $1/2$-cup (125ml) glasses. Cover and refrigerate for 6 hours or until the mousse is firm.

4 Serve the mousse topped with the raspberries.

TIPS

- If the ricotta is too cold and the melted chocolate becomes too firm, simply microwave for 15 seconds to soften before folding in the egg whites.
- Dutch-process cocoa powder is darker than natural cocoa powder and has a mellower flavour. It goes through an alkalizing process when it is made, neutralizing the natural acidity of the cocoa beans.
- The mousse will keep, in the refrigerator, for up to 3 days.

White chocolate and caramel ripple mousse

SET | PREP + COOK TIME **20 MINUTES + REFRIGERATION** | SERVES **6**

With just a few ingredients and a small investment of time, you will create an irresistibly smooth white chocolate mousse that is lifted out of the ordinary by a swirl of delicious caramel – with tart raspberries to cap it all off.

200g white chocolate, finely chopped

³/₄ cup (180ml) double cream

3 egg whites

250g good-quality dark chocolate and caramel spread or 125g chocolate sandwich spread and 125g dulce de leche (see tips)

125g fresh raspberries

1   Put the white chocolate and cream in a small heatproof bowl over a small saucepan of gently simmering water (don't allow the base of the bowl to touch the water). Stir the chocolate-cream mixture until melted and smooth. Remove the bowl from the pan. Refrigerate for 30 minutes or until chilled and slightly thickened.

2   Using an electric mixer, beat the egg whites in a medium bowl until almost stiff peaks form. Fold into the cooled chocolate mixture.

3   Stir the chocolate and caramel spread while still in the jar to loosen the mixture. Add to the chocolate mixture; gently swirl through. Pour the mousse mixture into six ³/₄-cup (180ml) glasses. Refrigerate for 5 hours or until just set.

4   Serve the mousse topped with the raspberries.

TIPS

- We used Maggie Beer's dark chocolate and vino cotto caramel, available from specialist food stores, delis, and online – but it can be hard to find.
- You can swap the dark chocolate and caramel spread for Carnation Caramel filling instead, for a slightly softer mousse. Or try a thick balsamic chocolate dessert sauce, if you like.
- Top the mousse with sliced fresh figs instead of the raspberries.
- The mousse can be made up to a day ahead.

Chocolate sesame tarts

SET | PREP + COOK TIME **30 MINUTES + REFRIGERATION** | MAKES **6**

Finishing these tarts with a sprinkling of sesame seeds adds a wonderful toasty flavour and elevates this quick and easy chocolate dessert into something special. They add their signature aroma and with the orange zest ensure these treats smell as good as they look.

100g butter

200g plain sweet biscuits

1 small orange (180g)

200g dark chocolate (70% cocoa), broken into pieces

300ml double cream

2 tbsp caster sugar

1 tsp black sesame seeds, toasted

1 Melt the butter in a small saucepan or in a small heatproof bowl in the microwave. Process the biscuits until fine crumbs form. Stir in the melted butter. Divide the biscuit mixture among six 2cm deep, 8.5cm (base measure) fluted loose-bottomed tart tins. Press the mixture evenly over the bases and sides. Refrigerate for 30 minutes or until firm.

2 Meanwhile, finely grate the zest from the orange; you will need 2 teaspoons. Juice half of the orange; you will need $^1/_4$ cup (60ml) orange juice.

3 Put the chocolate, $^3/_4$ cup (180ml) of the cream and the sugar in a small saucepan. Stir over a low heat until melted and combined. Stir in the orange juice and 1 teaspoon of the zest. Pour the mixture into the tart shell cases. Refrigerate for 4 hours or until set.

4 Using an electric mixer, beat the remaining cream in a small bowl until soft peaks form.

5 Serve the tarts sprinkled with the sesame seeds and orange zest, topped with dollops of the remaining cream.

TIPS

- You can use white sesame seeds instead of black sesame seeds, if you prefer.
- Serve the tarts with coconut ice cream, if you like.

Churros with chilli chocolate

FRIED | PREP + COOK TIME **40 MINUTES** | SERVES **6**

Chocolate and chilli are one of those flavour pairings that can seem unexpected, but actually works to awaken all your taste buds. The chocolate dipping sauce here is zingy and rich, and a mouth-watering foil to the crisp churros. True indulgence doesn't get much better than this.

100g butter, coarsely chopped

1 cup (150g) plain flour, sifted

3 eggs

vegetable oil for deep-frying

1/3 cup (75g) caster sugar

1 tsp ground cinnamon

chilli chocolate sauce

300g dark chocolate (at least 70% cocoa), broken into pieces

30g butter

3/4 cup (180ml) double cream

pinch of Mexican chilli powder

1 To make the chilli chocolate sauce, break the chocolate into pieces into a medium heatproof bowl. Add the butter, cream, and chilli powder. Stir over a medium saucepan of simmering water (do not allow the water to touch the bottom of the bowl) until smooth. Set aside to keep warm.

2 Bring the butter and 1 cup (250ml) water to the boil in a medium saucepan. Add the sifted flour. Beat with a wooden spoon over a medium heat until the mixture comes away from the bottom and side of the pan and forms a smooth ball.

3 Transfer the mixture to a small bowl. Using an electric mixer, beat in the eggs, one at a time, on medium speed for about 1 minute or until the mixture becomes glossy. Allow to cool for 10 minutes.

4 Meanwhile, fill a large, wide saucepan with enough vegetable oil to come two-thirds of the way up the side; be careful not to overfill. Heat to 190°C/375°F (or until the oil sizzles when a small cube of bread is added). Spoon the mixture into a piping bag fitted with a 1cm fluted tube. Squeeze 15cm lengths of dough into the hot oil, cutting off the lengths with a sharp knife or scissors. Deep-fry about 4 strips at a time for about 2 minutes on each side or until lightly browned and crisp. Drain the churros on kitchen paper. Toss the hot churros in the combined sugar and cinnamon.

5 Serve immediately with small bowls or large cups of the warm chilli chocolate sauce for dipping.

Mocha, date, and cinnamon babka

BAKED | PREP + COOK TIME **1 HOUR 20 MINUTES + STANDING** | SERVES **8**

Using dates in this babka adds a caramel-like sweetness that complements and enhances the flavours of chocolate and coffee perfectly. It is best made on the day of serving.

10 soft fresh dates (250g), pitted, chopped

$1/3$ cup (80ml) coffee-flavoured liqueur

$3/4$ cup (180ml) lukewarm milk

4 tsp (14g) dried yeast

$1/2$ cup (110g) caster sugar

2 eggs, lightly beaten

1 egg yolk

3 cups (450g) white bread flour

3 tsp sea salt flakes

150g butter, softened, cubed, plus extra 40g

200g dark chocolate (70% cocoa), chopped

$1/2$ cup (125ml) double cream

2 tsp instant coffee granules

$1/4$ cup (35g) coarsely chopped walnuts

cinnamon chocolate filling

$2/3$ cup (70g) walnuts, lightly toasted, chopped

$1/3$ cup (75g) firmly packed soft light brown sugar

2 tsp ground cinnamon

150g dark chocolate (70% cocoa), chopped

TIP

If you don't have an electric mixer with a dough hook, in step 2, combine the ingredients in a large bowl with a wooden spoon to form a soft dough. Turn out onto a well-floured work surface and knead for 5 minutes until soft and elastic. Knead the butter piece by piece into the dough, kneading well after each addition, until the dough is smooth and elastic.

1 Combine the dates and liqueur in a small bowl. Set aside. In a separate small bowl, combine the milk, yeast, and 1 tablespoon of the sugar. Cover with cling film. Allow to stand in a warm place for 10 minutes or until frothy. Stir in the egg and egg yolk.

2 In a large bowl of an electric mixer fitted with a dough hook attachment, mix the flour, salt, remaining sugar, and yeast mixture on low speed until just combined. Increase the speed to medium; mix for 5 minutes until soft and elastic. With the motor operating, gradually add the 150g cubed butter, a piece at a time, making sure it is incorporated before adding the next piece. Mix until the dough is very smooth and elastic. Put in a large oiled bowl; cover with cling film. Allow to stand in a warm place (but not too warm or the dough will be greasy) for 1 hour or until doubled in size.

3 Meanwhile, preheat the oven to 180°C (160°C fan/350°F/Gas 4). Grease a non-stick 21cm kugelhopf tin well with butter. Drain the dates, reserving 2 tablespoons of the liqueur. Combine the filling ingredients in a bowl.

4 Punch down the dough with your fist. Knead lightly until smooth. On a floured piece of baking parchment, roll out into a rectangle 30cm x 40cm and 1cm thick. Spread the extra 40g butter on the dough. Sprinkle evenly with the soaked dates and the filling. Using the parchment as an aid, roll up firmly from one long side. Using a lightly oiled knife, cut the dough into 12 equal pieces (reshape into rounds). Place 7 pieces, cut-side out, around the outer side of the tin (use the middle pieces of the log for this). Put the remaining pieces of the log around the inner ring of the tin, overlapping slightly. Cover with cling film. Allow to stand in a warm place for 45 minutes or until the dough has almost doubled in size. Bake on the lowest oven shelf for 40 minutes or until cooked through. Leave in the tin for 5 minutes, before turning out onto a wire rack to cool slightly.

5 Put the chocolate, cream, coffee granules, and reserved liqueur in a medium microwave-safe bowl. Microwave on HIGH (100%) for 1 minute or until melted and smooth. Allow to cool for 10 minutes. Serve the warm babka drizzled with the warm mocha sauce and topped with the walnuts.

Warm choc-nut brownie with coffee crème anglaise

BAKED | PREP + COOK TIME **1 HOUR** | SERVES **8**

These brownies are made extra special with the addition of the light but delicious coffee-flavoured crème anglaise. A thin pouring custard, crème anglaise is often used with cakes and puddings, as well as with fruit desserts.

275g dark chocolate, finely chopped, plus extra 100g, coarsely chopped (see tips)

150g butter, chopped

$^2/_3$ cup (150g) caster sugar

2 eggs, lightly beaten

1 cup (150g) plain flour, sifted

$^1/_2$ cup (75g) self-raising flour, sifted

$^2/_3$ cup (90g) coarsely chopped unsalted macadamias, lightly toasted

100g milk chocolate, coarsely chopped

coffee crème anglaise

2 cups (500ml) double cream

1 tbsp instant coffee granules

4 egg yolks

$^1/_4$ cup (55g) caster sugar

1 Preheat the oven to 170°C (150°C fan/325°F/Gas 3). Grease a shallow 20cm square cake tin. Line the bottom with baking parchment.

2 Stir the dark chocolate and butter in a medium saucepan over a low heat until smooth. Remove from the heat.

3 Stir the sugar, then the beaten eggs, into the chocolate mixture. Fold in the combined sifted flours, then the macadamias, milk chocolate, and extra 100g coarsely chopped dark chocolate. Spread the brownie mixture over the bottom of the prepared cake tin.

4 Bake for 35 minutes or until a skewer inserted into the centre comes out with moist crumbs. Allow to stand in the tin for 10 minutes.

5 Meanwhile, to make the coffee crème anglaise, bring the cream to the boil in a medium saucepan. Remove from the heat. Stir in the coffee until dissolved. Whisk together the egg yolks and sugar in a medium bowl until creamy. Gradually whisk in the warm cream mixture. Return the mixture to the pan. Stir over a medium-high heat, without boiling, until the custard thickens and coats the back of a spoon. Strain the custard into a medium jug.

6 Serve the warm brownie accompanied by the coffee crème anglaise.

TIPS

- These brownies will be only as good as the chocolate used. The more cocoa solids it contains, the more intense the chocolate taste. Aim for a dark chocolate containing between 50% and 70% cocoa solids. Chocolate containing a lower percentage of cocoa solids means more added sugar and fat.
- The brownies can be made up to 3 days ahead. Store them in an airtight container. Reheat for 30 seconds in the microwave.

Chocolate self-saucing pudding with quick banana 'ice cream'

BAKED AND FROZEN | PREP + COOK TIME **50 MINUTES + FREEZING** | SERVES **6**

Due to their high pectin content, bananas naturally have a creamy texture. This is especially noticeable when banana is frozen and blended into a smooth and satisfyingly creamy quick frozen dessert such as the one here.

You will need to freeze the bananas a day ahead

1 cup (150g) self-raising flour

$^1/_3$ cup (35g) Dutch-process cocoa powder, plus extra, to dust

1 tsp ground cinnamon

1 tsp ground ginger

$^1/_2$ tsp ground nutmeg

pinch of salt

$^3/_4$ cup (165g) raw caster sugar

1 egg

2 tsp vanilla bean paste

$^1/_2$ cup (125ml) milk

2 tbsp almond butter

$^3/_4$ cup (165g) firmly packed light soft brown sugar

quick banana ice cream

500g bananas, chopped, frozen (see tips)

1 tsp vanilla bean paste

2 tbsp pure maple syrup

2 tbsp almond butter

1 To make the quick banana ice cream, process the frozen banana until coarsely chopped. Add the vanilla bean paste, maple syrup, and almond butter. Process until smooth. Spoon into a $2^1/_2$-cup (625ml) freezerproof container. Freeze for 2 hours before scooping.

2 Preheat the oven to 180°C (160°C fan/350°F/Gas 4). Grease a 7-cup (1.75-litre) round ovenproof dish. Place on a baking tray.

3 Sift the flour, half of the cocoa powder, the spices, and salt into a medium bowl. Stir in the caster sugar. Whisk together the egg, vanilla bean paste, milk, and almond butter in a small jug. Pour over the dry ingredients; stir until combined. Spoon into the prepared ovenproof dish.

4 Combine the soft brown sugar with the remaining 2 tablespoons cocoa powder. Sprinkle over the top of the chocolate batter. Slowly pour $1^1/_3$ cups (330ml) boiling water over the back of a metal spoon to cover the pudding.

5 Bake the pudding for 35 minutes or until the pudding bounces back when pressed gently in the centre.

6 Serve immediately with scoops of the banana ice cream, dusted with extra cocoa powder.

TIPS

▪ You will need about $2^1/_2$ large bananas or 3 medium bananas. For accuracy, peel the bananas first, then weigh. For the best flavour, use just-ripe bananas.

▪ Top the servings with finely grated chocolate and dried unsprayed rose petals or buds, if you like.

Stacked mocha blackout cake

BAKED | PREP + COOK TIME **1 HOUR 10 MINUTES + COOLING** | SERVES **10**

With its moist, dense crumb and slathering of intensely chocolaty soured cream icing, this cake transforms the classic combination of chocolate and coffee into a special-occasion dessert that will excite your guests and definitely satisfy any sweet cravings.

1^1/$_2$ tbsp instant coffee granules

1^1/$_4$ cups (275g) caster sugar

1^1/$_4$ cups (275g) soft light brown sugar

2 cups (300g) plain flour, sifted

1 cup (100g) Dutch-process cocoa powder (see tips)

1 tsp bicarbonate of soda

2 tsp baking powder

^{2}/$_3$ cup (160ml) vegetable oil

3 eggs, lightly beaten

1 cup (250ml) buttermilk

unsprayed fresh flowers, to decorate

soured cream chocolate icing

2 cups (320g) icing sugar

^{3}/$_4$ cup (75g) Dutch-process cocoa powder

200g unsalted butter, chopped, softened

200g dark chocolate (at least 70% cocoa), melted, cooled

250g soured cream

1   Preheat the oven to 160°C (140°C fan/325°F/Gas 3). Grease 2 deep 20cm round cake tins. Line the bottoms and sides with baking parchment.

2   Put ^{1}/$_2$ cup (125ml) boiling water and the coffee granules in a small bowl. Stir until dissolved. Combine the sugars in a large bowl. Add the sifted flour, cocoa, bicarbonate of soda, and baking powder. Add the vegetable oil, eggs, buttermilk, and coffee mixture. Whisk to combine. Divide the mixture evenly between the prepared tins (see tips).

3   Bake the cakes for 50 minutes or until a skewer inserted into the centre comes out clean. Allow to stand in the tins for 10 minutes, before turning out onto wire racks to cool.

4   Meanwhile, to make the soured cream chocolate icing, sift the icing sugar and cocoa powder together into a medium bowl. Add the butter. Beat with an electric mixer for 4 minutes or until paler and creamy. Combine the chocolate and soured cream in a separate bowl. Add to the butter mixture. Beat for a further 2 minutes or until well combined.

5   Place one of the cakes, right-side down, on a serving plate. Top with ^{3}/$_4$ cup (185ml) of the chocolate icing. Spread evenly. Top with the second cake, right-side up, and use the remaining icing to spread over the top and side of the cake in large swirls. Decorate with fresh flowers.

TIPS

• Darker and more mellow than natural cocoa powder, Dutch-process cocoa powder is washed when it is made to neutralize cocoa's natural acidity. This means it does not react with bicarbonate of soda, so you need to use baking powder as a raising agent when making cakes such as this one.

• After putting the cake mixture in the cake tins, weigh them to ensure it's distributed evenly.

NUTS AND CARAMEL

With treats ranging from unctuous caramel
fudge to crunchy-topped crumbles, nuts and
caramel reign supreme here – whether a
fundamental element or a final flourish.

Choc-caramel ice cream waffle cake

FROZEN | PREP + COOK TIME **30 MINUTES + FREEZING** | SERVES **10**

Easy-to-source and ready-made ingredients are transformed here into an almost architectural dessert of irresistible scrumptiousness. This is a great choice for those times when you don't feel like 'cooking' and is sure to impress when you bring it to the table.

You will need to start this recipe a day ahead

720g plain or chocolate chip Belgian waffles

2 x 380g cans Carnation Caramel filling

500g cream cheese, chopped, softened

2 x 50g chocolate-coated honeycomb bars, coarsely chopped (see tips)

3 oranges (720g)

2 mandarins (200g) (see tip)

1 cup (250ml) bottled salted caramel sauce

1 Grease a 24cm springform cake tin. Line the bottom and side with baking parchment, extending the parchment 3cm above the edge.

2 Trim the waffles straight lengthways, following the natural waffle pattern. Place about 5 waffles, lengthways, around the inside edge of the prepared tin to create a collar. Trim the remaining waffles crossways on both sides to level. Arrange, trimming as needed, so that they cover the bottom of the pan and you have a well in the centre for the filling.

3 Using an electric mixer, beat together the caramel filling and cream cheese in a large bowl until smooth and combined. Fold in half the chopped honeycomb bars. Spoon the mixture into the waffle-lined tin. Smooth the surface to level. Freeze overnight.

4 The next day, peel the oranges, removing any pith. Thinly slice crossways, then cut into wedges. Peel and segment the mandarins.

5 To serve, top the ice cream waffle cake with the oranges, mandarins, and remaining honeycomb bar. Drizzle with a little of the salted caramel sauce. Serve cut into slices, drizzled with the remaining caramel sauce.

TIPS

- If you like, you can use the recipe for choc-dipped salted honeycomb on page 114 instead of purchased bars. Just remember to make it a day ahead, and store in an airtight container in a cool, dry place until needed for assembling on the day of serving.
- If fresh mandarins are unavailable, substitute with 2 oranges instead.

Macadamia Florentine ice cream sandwiches

BAKED AND FROZEN | PREP + COOK TIME **45 MINUTES PLUS COOLING + FREEZING** | SERVES **6**

Florentines are chockful of nuts and dried fruit. The biscuits used here echo this with an evocative topping of macadamias, cranberries, and glacé ginger. If you're short on time but like the idea of this dessert, use ready-made Florentines to sandwich with instead.

80g butter

³/₄ cup (165g) caster sugar

¹/₄ tsp sea salt flakes

300ml double cream

³/₄ cup (115g) plain flour

¹/₄ tsp ground ginger

¹/₄ tsp sea salt flakes

³/₄ cup (105g) coarsely chopped macadamias

¹/₄ cup (35g) dried cranberries

¹/₄ cup (60g) glacé ginger, coarsely chopped

150g dark chocolate (70% cocoa), coarsely chopped

6 scoops of slightly softened vanilla ice cream (750ml)

1 Preheat the oven to 160°C (140°C fan/325°F/Gas 3). Line 2 large baking trays with baking parchment. Place another large baking tray on the top shelf of the oven to prevent the Florentines from browning too much.

2 Melt the butter in a medium saucepan over a medium heat. Add the sugar, salt flakes, and cream. Cook, stirring, for 2 minutes or until well combined. Fold in the flour and ground ginger; be careful not to overmix. Remove from the heat.

3 Once the mixture is cool enough to handle, working in batches, drop 2 tablespoons of the mixture on top of each other onto the prepared trays, leaving a 3cm gap between each one. The mixture should spread to an 8cm round and make 12 rounds in total. Sprinkle the macadamias, cranberries, and glacé ginger evenly over the Florentines.

4 Bake the Florentines for 22 minutes or until light golden in the centre, rotating the trays during cooking so that the biscuits brown evenly. Allow to cool on the trays.

5 Microwave the chocolate in a small bowl on HIGH (100%) in 30-second bursts, stirring well, until melted. Allow to cool slightly. Set aside.

6 Scoop the slightly softened ice cream into 6 large balls. Sandwich 1 scoop between 2 Florentines, placing the biscuits topping-side out. Gently press the Florentines together to form even sandwiches. Dip each sandwich a third of the way down into the melted chocolate. Arrange on a tray. Freeze until the chocolate sets.

7 Serve the ice cream sandwiches straight from the freezer.

TIPS

- The Florentines can be made up to 3 days ahead. Store in an airtight container or freeze for up to 3 months.
- Use honey ice cream instead of vanilla to fill the sandwiches, if you like.

Peanut butter puddings

BAKED | PREP + COOK TIME **35 MINUTES** | MAKES **6**

Classic comfort food in a dish, these puddings make for sweet, satisfying succour on a wintry night – or any night, really. Why limit their temptation? Using crunchy peanut butter instead of smooth adds wonderful texture, with crunches and pops of peanut goodness in every bite.

6 eggs

75g dark chocolate (70% cocoa)

100g crystallized ginger

$^1/_2$ cup (110g) caster sugar

325g crunchy peanut butter (see tips)

$^1/_3$ cup (80ml) boiling water

$^1/_2$ tsp fine sea salt

$^2/_3$ cup (160ml) double cream

2 tsp icing sugar, sifted

1 Preheat the oven to 190°C (170°C fan/375°F/Gas 5). Grease six $^3/_4$-cup (180ml) ramekins or ovenproof dishes.

2 Separate the eggs. Put the egg whites in a small cup or bowl and the yolks in the bowl of an electric mixer. Finely chop 50g of the chocolate. Finely chop the crystallized ginger. Reserve 2 tablespoons to serve.

3 Add the caster sugar to the egg yolks. Beat with electric mixer until light and creamy. Blend the peanut butter and the $^1/_3$ cup (80ml) boiling water separately in a cup or small jug. Add to the egg yolk mixture. Beat until combined. Transfer the mixture to a large bowl. Stir in the chopped chocolate, crystallized ginger, and sea salt.

4 Wash and dry the bowl of the electric mixer. Add the egg whites to the clean bowl. Beat with the electric mixer until soft peaks form. Fold one-third of the egg whites into the pudding mixture, in 3 batches, until combined. Spoon the mixture into the ramekins.

5 Bake the puddings for 20 minutes or until gooey in the centre.

6 Meanwhile, finely grate remaining chocolate or shave with a peeler. Using an electric mixer, beat together the cream and sifted icing sugar until soft peaks form.

7 Serve the puddings immediately, topped with the cream, the reserved ginger, and the reserved grated chocolate.

TIPS

- Instead of the crystallized ginger, use the same weight of chopped fresh dates or dried figs.
- It is important to use a sweetened peanut butter. Natural peanut butters won't yield the same result.
- When washing the bowl in step 4, make sure that it is clean of any oils and dried well. Fat and moisture will prevent the egg whites from forming soft peaks.
- Serve the puddings drizzled with dulce de leche or topped with vanilla ice cream, if you like.

Orange crème caramel with toffeed hazelnuts

BAKED | PREP + COOK TIME **1 HOUR + OVERNIGHT REFRIGERATION** | SERVES **12**

Sometimes you just need to go with a retro favourite, and this crème caramel with a twist fits the bill. The custard base is made with condensed milk in the style of a Latin American flan, while the strong, deep flavour of the toffeed hazelnuts pairs particularly well with the orange.

You will need to start this recipe a day ahead

cooking oil spray for greasing

1$\frac{1}{4}$ cups (275g) caster sugar

2 large oranges (600g)

395g sweetened condensed milk

600ml whole milk

6 eggs

$\frac{1}{2}$ cup (70g) skinless toasted hazelnuts, coarsely chopped

thick double cream, to serve (optional)

TIPS

- For best results, use the fan function on your oven to cook the crème caramel. Don't forget that this means you need to cook at an oven temperature 20 degrees lower than for conventional cooking.
- Skinless toasted hazelnuts are in the baking section of supermarkets. Alternatively, toast the hazelnuts in the oven for 10 minutes, then wrap in a clean tea towel. Allow to steam for a minute, then rub off the skins with the hazelnuts still wrapped in the tea towel.
- You can use other nuts such as almonds or cashews instead of the hazelnuts.

1 Lightly coat an 18cm square cake tin with cooking oil spray.

2 Put 1 cup (220g) of the caster sugar and $\frac{1}{2}$ cup (125ml) water in a small saucepan. Stir over a medium heat without boiling until the sugar dissolves. Bring to the boil, without stirring (to prevent sugar crystals forming on the side of the pan, brush the side with cold water). Boil for 8 minutes or until golden brown. Pour the caramel into the cake tin. Carefully swirl around the tin to coat the bottom and sides.

3 Preheat the oven to 160°C (140°C fan/325°F/Gas 3) (see tip). Use a zesting tool to cut the zest from 1 of the oranges in long, thin strips; reserve. Finely grate the zest of the other orange (you will need 2 tablespoons).

4 Whisk together the milks, eggs, and 1 tablespoon of the grated orange zest in a large bowl until combined. Strain the mixture directly onto the caramel in the tin. Place the tin in a roasting pan. Add enough hot water to the roasting pan to come halfway up the sides of the cake tin.

5 Bake the crème caramel for 45 minutes. The mixture will still be wobbly in the centre. Carefully remove the tin from the water. Using your fingers, gently pull the custard away from the sides; this will prevent the top of the custard from cracking as it cools. Refrigerate overnight.

6 Line a baking tray with baking parchment. Put the remaining $\frac{1}{4}$ cup (55g) caster sugar and 1 tablespoon water in a small heavy-based saucepan. Cook, stirring, over a low heat until the sugar dissolves. Add the remaining grated orange zest; increase the heat to high. Cook without stirring for 6 minutes or until golden. Remove the pan from the heat. Quickly stir in the hazelnuts to coat. Pour onto the lined tray. Leave to cool completely. Break or coarsely chop into pieces.

7 Place a serving platter with a lip right-side down on the cake tin. Quickly invert the pan so the caramel drops onto the platter. Remove the tin. Serve the crème caramel topped with the reserved strips of orange zest, toffeed hazelnuts, and dollops of thick cream, if you like.

Little mandarin and almond crater cakes

BAKED | PREP + COOK TIME **3 HOURS + COOLING** | MAKES **12**

The little craters in these moist, citrus-dense almond cakes create the ideal little vessels to spoon thick yogurt, custard, or even ice cream into for serving. Candied zest tops off these mini mandarin fests with a zesty flourish.

4 large mandarins (1kg)

400g flaked natural almonds

6 eggs

1½ cups (330g) caster sugar

1½ tsp baking powder

1 cup (280g) Greek-style yogurt, to serve

TIPS

- You can also make the cakes in two 6-hole (³/₄-cup/180ml) Texas (jumbo) muffin tins, baking for 35 minutes, following the instructions.
- These cakes have a high moisture content from using whole processed mandarins, and so benefit from being cooked with the fan on. The circulating air helps to form a better crust on the cakes.
- The mandarin purée and candied zest can be made a day ahead. Store the purée in the fridge and the zest at room temperature.
- Add 1 teaspoon vanilla extract to the cake mixture, if you like.

1 Place 2 whole mandarins in a medium saucepan with enough water to cover. Bring to the boil. Reduce the heat to low. Simmer for 2 hours, adding more water as needed to keep the mandarins covered at all times. Remove from the water; allow to cool. Split open; remove and discard the seeds. Process the mandarins (including the peel) to a purée.

2 Preheat the oven to 180°C (160°C fan/350°F/Gas 4).

3 Divide 300g of the almonds between 2 baking trays. Roast for 7 minutes, stirring halfway through the cooking time, or until golden. Allow to cool, then process to fine crumbs.

4 If using a conventional oven, switch to its fan function (see tips); reduce the oven temperature to 160°C fan-forced (140°C fan/325°F/Gas 3 if fan/gas throughout). Line the bottoms and sides of a 12-hole (³/₄-cup/180ml) loose-bottomed mini sandwich tin with baking parchment.

5 Using an electric mixer, beat the eggs and 1 cup (220g) of the sugar in a large bowl for 10 minutes or until thick, pale, and tripled in volume. Fold in the ground almonds, mandarin purée, and baking powder. Spoon into the cake tin holes, filling to the rim. Top with the remaining almonds.

6 Bake the cakes for 30 minutes or until the cakes look set and have sunk slightly in the centre and come away from the edge. Leave in the tin for 10 minutes. Transfer to a wire rack to cool completely.

7 Meanwhile, remove the zest and any pith from the remaining mandarins. Slice the zest into thin strips. Process the mandarin segments until smooth. Pour the purée through a sieve over a measuring cup; discard the pulp. You should have about ²/₃ cup (160ml) juice. Top up with water to make 1 cup (250ml). Put the juice mixture and remaining ½ cup (110g) sugar in a medium frying pan over a low heat. Stir without boiling until the sugar dissolves. Add the zest. Boil for 5 minutes or until golden. Transfer the zest to a baking tray lined with baking parchment. Allow to cool. Serve the cakes with the candied mandarin zest and yogurt.

Almond crumble tray-baked fruit

BAKED | PREP + COOK TIME **1 HOUR 20 MINUTES** | SERVES **6**

The humble crumble is a very versatile and forgiving dessert. Swap and use your favourite
fruit such as apple, raspberries, or plums within the same quantities – just be sure to adjust
the cooking time and cook until the fruit is tender.

5 Beurre Bosc pears (1.2kg)

250g blackberries, plus extra, to serve

2 large oranges (600g)

¹/₃ cup (75g) caster sugar

75g butter

1 cup (120g) slivered almonds

1 cup (90g) rolled oats

1 Preheat the oven to 200°C (180°C fan/400°F/Gas 6).

2 Halve and core the pears. Cut each half into 4 wedges. Arrange the pears
and blackberries in a 2-litre (8-cup) ovenproof dish.

3 Remove the zest from 1 of the oranges using a zesting tool. Finely grate
the zest from the second orange. Reserve the zests separately. Squeeze
the oranges; you will need ³/₄ cup (180ml) orange juice. Pour the juice
over the pears in the dish. Sprinkle with half of the sugar and the first
batch of reserved strips of zest. Stir to coat.

4 Bake the fruit, stirring occasionally, for 45 minutes or until the pears are
almost tender.

5 Meanwhile, finely chop the butter. Put the almonds, rolled oats,
remaining sugar, and chopped butter in a medium bowl. Using your
fingertips, rub the butter into the almond mixture until the mixture
resembles coarse crumbs.

6 Scatter the almond crumbs over the pear mixture. Bake for 15 minutes or
until the crumble is golden. Serve topped with extra blackberries and the
second batch of reserved grated zest.

TIPS

- Serve with scoops of vanilla bean ice cream.
- Use frozen berries when fresh blackberries
are not in season.

Salted caramels

STOVETOP | PREP + COOK TIME **30 MINUTES + COOLING** | MAKES **40**

Adding sea salt to these simple caramels turns them into a taste sensation in your mouth.
And making your own caramels is not a daunting process – just be patient and make sure that
the syrup mixture reaches the right temperature before taking it off the heat.

1½ cups (330g) caster sugar
1½ cups (375ml) whipping or double cream
¼ cup (90g) glucose syrup
2 tsp sea salt flakes

1   Grease a 20cm square cake tin. Line the bottom and sides with baking
    parchment, extending the parchment 5cm over the sides.

2   Stir the sugar, cream, and glucose syrup in a medium saucepan over
    a medium heat until the sugar dissolves. Bring to the boil. Boil until
    the mixture reaches 120°C (248°F) on a cooking thermometer (firm-ball
    stage). Sprinkle in 1 teaspoon of the salt flakes; do not stir.

3   Pour the caramel into the lined pan. Sprinkle with the remaining
    1 teaspoon salt. Allow to cool.

4   Use a warm, oiled sharp knife to cut the caramel into squares. Wrap in
    waxed paper or serve in little paper cases.

Salted caramels variations

Home-made caramels can be hard to resist, and the examples here are no exceptions. Make them as festive treats or to give as gifts to family and friends - or make them simply for the sheer indulgence of enjoying them yourself, no special occasion attached.

Almond and chocolate caramels

Grease an 18cm x 28cm shallow rectangular cake tin. Make the salted caramels as described on page 98, adding $1\frac{1}{2}$ cups (240g) roasted natural almonds and 75g finely chopped dark chocolate with 1 teaspoon of the sea salt flakes once the mixture reaches 110°C (240°F) on a cooking thermometer. Stir until the mixture reaches 120°C (248°F). Pour into the prepared tin. Sprinkle with the remaining 1 teaspoon sea salt flakes. Allow to cool, then cut into triangles. The caramels will harden as they cool.

Macadamia salted caramels

Grease an 18cm x 28cm shallow rectangular cake tin. Make the salted caramels as described on page 98, adding $1\frac{1}{2}$ cups (225g) unsalted roasted macadamias with 1 teaspoon of the sea salt flakes once the mixture reaches 120°C (248°F) on a cooking thermometer. Pour into the prepared tin. Sprinkle with the remaining 1 teaspoon sea salt flakes. Allow to cool. Using your hands, break the caramels into pieces.

Eggnog caramels

Make the salted caramels as described on page 98, omitting the salt and adding $1\frac{1}{2}$ teaspoons ground cinnamon, $\frac{1}{4}$ teaspoon ground nutmeg, a pinch of ground cloves, 1 teaspoon vanilla bean paste, and 2 tablespoons white rum to the pan with the sugar. Continue as directed in the recipe.

Earl Grey caramels

Infuse 2 Earl Grey teabags in $\frac{3}{4}$ cup (180ml) boiling water. Remove the teabags, pressing with the back of a spoon to release all the liquid. Make the salted caramels as described on page 98, omitting the salt and adding the tea to the sugar, cream, and glucose syrup in the pan. Continue as directed in the recipe.

Coconut banoffee tart

SET | PREP + COOK TIME **25 MINUTES + REFRIGERATION** | SERVES **8**

The banoffee pie gets an Australian makeover with the addition of sweet and caramelized Anzac biscuits in the crust. Anzac biscuits, made with rolled oats, golden syrup, and often coconut, are an institution in Australia and New Zealand, with long historical associations.

300g Anzac biscuits or other crunchy sweet oat biscuits such as Hobnobs

150g butter

500g mascarpone

380g Carnation Caramel filling

1/4 tsp sea salt flakes

2 large bananas (460g), just ripe

2 tbsp caster sugar

1/4 cup (20g) roasted coconut chips

1 Grease a 24cm loose-bottomed round tart tin.

2 Process the biscuits to fine crumbs. Melt 125g of the butter in a small saucepan or in a heatproof bowl in the microwave. Stir in the biscuit crumbs. Press over the base and side of the tart tin. Place on a baking tray. Refrigerate for 1 hour or overnight until firm.

3 Put 250g of mascarpone, the caramel filling, and salt flakes in a large bowl. Whisk until smooth and soft peaks form. Spread over the biscuit base. Refrigerate for 2 hours.

4 Melt the remaining butter in a large non-stick frying pan over a high heat. Thickly slice the bananas lengthways. Sprinkle with the sugar. Cook the bananas for 30 seconds on each side or until caramelized (see tips).

5 Top the tart with the caramelized banana and coconut chips. Serve with the remaining mascarpone.

TIPS

- Make a batch of your own Anzac biscuits to use in this recipe, if you like. This way you will keep the characteristic golden syrup flavour in the base.
- The biscuit base can be made a day ahead. Refrigerate until needed.
- The tart can be made to the end of step 3 the day before. Cover and refrigerate. Cook the bananas just before serving.
- You can use 3 or 4 finger bananas instead of regular bananas.
- If you have one, you can use a kitchen blowtorch to caramelize the bananas in step 4.

Spanish caramel orange cake

BAKED | PREP + COOK TIME **1 HOUR 25 MINUTES + STANDING** | SERVES **8**

Dulce de leche, the Latin American spreadable caramel, is made by simmering sweetened milk until thick and caramelized. Used here in combination with cream as a filling and topping, it transforms a simple butter cake into an afternoon-tea delight.

320g unsalted butter, softened,
plus extra for greasing

2 tsp vanilla bean paste

2 cups (440g) caster sugar, plus extra 2 tbsp

4 eggs, at room temperature

2½ cups (375g) self-raising flour, sifted

½ cup (75g) plain flour, sifted

1⅓ cup (330ml) milk

1 tbsp lemon juice

¾ cup (180ml) strained orange juice

250g mascarpone

1 cup (310g) dulce de leche

4 blood oranges (960g), peeled, thinly sliced

¼ cup (20g) flaked almonds, roasted

1   Preheat the oven to 160°C (140°C fan/325°F/Gas 3). Grease 2 deep 20cm round cake tins. Line the bottoms and sides of the tins with baking parchment, extending the paper 5cm above the sides.

2   Using an electric mixer, beat the butter, vanilla bean paste, and the 2 cups (440g) caster sugar in a medium bowl until light and fluffy. Add the eggs, one at a time, beating until just combined between additions. Transfer the mixture to a large bowl. Fold in the combined sifted flours and milk in 2 batches. Divide the mixture evenly between the 2 prepared tins, spreading over the bottom of each tin.

3   Bake the cakes for 50 minutes or until a skewer inserted into the centre comes out clean. Leave the cakes in the tins for 10 minutes, before turning onto a wire rack to cool completely.

4   Put the extra 2 tablespoons caster sugar and the lemon and orange juices in a medium saucepan. Stir over a medium heat until the sugar dissolves. Bring to the boil. Boil for 5 minutes or until the syrup thickens slightly and reduces to ⅓ cup (80ml). Transfer the syrup to a small jug. Cool quickly by placing in a bowl of iced water for 10 minutes.

5   Meanwhile, whisk together the mascarpone and dulce de leche in a medium bowl until soft peaks form.

6   Using a sharp knife, split each cooled cake in half horizontally, so that you have 4 layers. Place one cake layer, cut-side up, on a cake plate. Brush with 1 tablespoon of the cooled orange syrup. Spread with one-quarter of the dulce de leche cream. Repeat the layers 3 more times with the remaining cake, orange syrup, and dulce de leche cream.

7   Top the cake with half of the sliced oranges and sprinkle with the almonds. Serve the cake accompanied by the remaining orange slices.

TIPS

• You can substitute the same amount of vanilla extract for the vanilla bean paste.

• Dulce de leche is available in jars from delis and supermarkets. You can use Carnation Caramel filling instead, if you like.

Sugar and spice almonds

ROASTED | PREP + COOK TIME **30 MINUTES + COOLING** | MAKES **5 CUPS**

These sweet, spicy almonds are great as a snack or to serve guests. You can even present them as gifts, wrapped in a gift bag with a decorative ribbon tied at the top. The cinnamon sugar caramelizes slightly in the oven, adding a crisp coating to the crunchy almonds.

1$^{1}/_{2}$ cups (240g) pure icing sugar
1$^{1}/_{2}$ tbsp ground cinnamon
5 cups (800g) natural almonds

1 Preheat the oven to 180°C (160°C fan/350°F/Gas 4). Line 2 baking trays with baking parchment.

2 Sift the sugar and cinnamon together twice into a medium bowl. Put the almonds in a colander. Rinse under cold water. Tip the wet almonds onto the prepared baking trays. Sift the cinnamon mixture over the almonds. Toss to coat.

3 Roast for 20 minutes, stirring halfway through the cooking time, or until fragrant and browned. Allow to cool on the trays; they will become crisp on cooling. Separate the almonds, then store in airtight jars or pack in cellophane or similar gift bags, sealing the bags tightly at the top to ensure the nuts retain their freshness.

Pear fritters with raspberry and rose syrup

FRIED | PREP + COOK TIME **20 MINUTES** | SERVES **4**

Using purchased pancake mixture is a speedy and failproof hack for these tender-crisp fritters. The textural and flavour contrasts between the crisp batter coating and sweet, fragrant pears are an object lesson in perfect pairings, finished with the crunch of pistachios.

200g purchased pancake mixture (see tip)

1/4 cup (60ml) vegetable oil

2 firm pears (460g), peeled, cored, thickly sliced

2–3 tbsp fresh raspberries, plus extra, to serve

1/3 cup (115g) runny honey

1 tsp rosewater

1/3 cup (95g) Greek-style yogurt

2 tbsp coarsely chopped raw pistachios

1 Make the pancake batter according to the instructions. Pour the batter into a small bowl.

2 Heat 1 tablespoon of the vegetable oil in a large frying pan over a medium heat.

3 Add the pear slices to the pancake batter. Cook the coated pear slices in batches, adding more oil in between, for 2 minutes on each side or until golden. Drain on kitchen paper.

4 Put the raspberries, honey, and rosewater in a small bowl. Mash with a fork to combine and crush.

5 Divide the warm fritters among 4 serving bowls. Top with the yogurt and raspberry rose syrup. Sprinkle with the pistachios.

TIPS

- We used a bottled pancake mixture designed to be mixed and shaken in the bottle.
- Any leftover pancake batter can be stored in the fridge and used the following day.

Amaretti crumbles with apple and cherry

BAKED | PREP + COOK TIME **35 MINUTES** | SERVES **4**

Almond-flavoured amaretti complement the cherries beautifully here, transforming the humble crumble into something just that little bit special. If you aren't a fan of amaretti biscuits, you can use another biscuit instead. Shortbread works equally well in this recipe.

5 apples (750g), peeled, cored, thickly sliced

¼ cup (55g) caster sugar

½ tsp mixed spice

1½ cups (225g) frozen seedless cherries

125g amaretti biscuits, crushed

¼ cup (30g) ground almonds

¼ cup (35g) slivered almonds

¼ cup (35g) plain flour

80g cold butter, finely chopped,
plus extra for greasing

vanilla ice cream, to serve (optional)

1 Preheat the oven to 200°C (180°C fan/400°F/Gas 6). Grease four 1¼-cup (310ml) ovenproof dishes.

2 Combine the apples, sugar, 2 tablespoons water, and mixed spice in a medium saucepan. Cook, covered, over a medium heat for about 5 minutes or until the apples are just tender. Remove from the heat. Stir in the cherries. Divide the mixture among the prepared dishes.

3 Meanwhile, combine the crushed biscuits, ground almonds, slivered almonds, and flour in a medium bowl. Rub in the cold butter. Sprinkle the mixture evenly over the apple-cherry mixture.

4 Place the dishes on a baking tray. Bake for about 20 minutes or until browned. Serve with ice cream, if you like.

TIP

You can use any frozen berry you like, instead of the cherries.

Skillet cake with tahini maple caramel pears

BAKED | PREP + COOK TIME **40 MINUTES** | SERVES **6**

Roasted pears and maple syrup make this recipe a sublime choice for an autumnal weekend brunch. It can also serve as an everyday family dessert, especially when it takes advantage of seasonal fruit. Quick and easy, it's even more perfect with vanilla ice cream.

1¹/₂ cups (225g) self-raising flour

¹/₄ tsp bicarbonate of soda

2 tsp ground cinnamon

¹/₃ cup (90g) tahini

²/₃ cup (160ml) maple syrup

2 eggs, lightly beaten

1¹/₂ cups (375ml) buttermilk

50g butter

3 firm Beurre Bosc pears (690g), unpeeled, each cut into 6 wedges

2 tbsp lemon juice

toasted sesame seeds, to serve

1 Preheat the oven to 220°C (200°C fan/425°F/Gas 7). Place a 26cm (top measurement) ovenproof skillet in the oven to preheat.

2 Put the flour, bicarbonate of soda, and 1 teaspoon of the cinnamon in a large bowl. Add 2 tablespoons each of the tahini and maple syrup, then the egg and buttermilk. Whisk until combined.

3 Heat 30g of the butter in a large frying pan over a medium heat. Add the pears. Cook, turning occasionally, for 8 minutes or until browned and almost tender. Add the remaining 1 teaspoon cinnamon, tahini, and maple syrup, then the lemon juice. Stir gently until combined. Cook, over a low heat, stirring occasionally, for 5 minutes or until the pears are tender and the sauce is thickened. Set aside.

4 Meanwhile, carefully but quickly remove the hot skillet from the oven. Add the remaining 20g butter; swirl to coat. Pour in the tahini-maple mixture. Smooth the surface. Bake for 15 minutes or until puffed and browned, and a skewer inserted into the centre comes out clean.

5 To serve, top the hot skillet cake with the tahini maple caramel pears, and sprinkle with the sesame seeds.

TIP

You could also use this mixture to make individual puffed pancakes, if you like.

Warm chocolate caramel pavlovas

STOVETOP AND BAKED | PREP + COOK TIME **1 HOUR + COOLING** | SERVES **4**

Set to impress, this meringue recipe foregoes the more typical fresh fruit and uses a delectable combination of banana, salted caramel, and chocolate instead. The honeycomb on the top is the icing on the cake – or pavlova, in this case.

2 egg whites

1 1/3 cups (215g) icing sugar

1/3 cup (80ml) boiling water

1 tbsp cocoa powder, sifted

1 cup (250ml) salted caramel dessert sauce

2 bananas (400g)

300ml extra thick double cream

50g chocolate-coated honeycomb bar, coarsely chopped

chocolate-dipped salted honeycomb

1 cup (220g) caster sugar

1/4 cup (60ml) pure maple syrup

2 tsp bicarbonate of soda, sifted

1 tsp sea salt flakes

melted milk chocolate for dipping

TIPS

• You can make the salted honeycomb in advance and store it in an airtight container until needed.

• If you don't have the time or inclination to make your own honeycomb, simply use a 50g purchased chocolate-coated honeycomb bar instead. Coarsely chop and use to top the pavlovas as in the picture.

1 To make the chocolate-dipped salted honeycomb, line a baking tray with baking parchment.

2 Stir together the caster sugar, maple syrup, and 1/4 cup (60ml) water in a medium heavy-based saucepan over a low heat until the sugar dissolves. Increase the heat to medium; boil, without stirring, for 8 minutes until the syrup is a dark golden honey colour or until it reaches 160°C/325°F (hard-crack stage) on a sugar thermometer.

3 Remove the pan the from heat; immediately stir in the sifted bicarbonate of soda – the syrup will froth. As soon as the last of the soda dissolves, carefully and quickly pour the honeycomb onto the prepared tray; don't spread the mixture or it will deflate. Sprinkle with the sea salt flakes; allow to cool to room temperature.

4 Break the cooled honeycomb into chunks. Dip the pieces into the milk chocolate and return to the tray. Allow to stand until set.

5 To make the pavlovas, preheat the oven to 180°C (160°C fan/350°F/Gas 4). Line a large baking tray with baking parchment.

6 Using an electric mixer, beat the egg whites, icing sugar, and 1/3 cup (80ml) boiling water in a small bowl for about 10 minutes or until firm peaks form.

7 Fold the sifted cocoa into the meringue. Drop 4 equal amounts of the mixture onto the lined tray. Use the back of a spoon to create a well in the centre of each mound. Bake for 25 minutes or until firm to the touch.

8 Meanwhile, heat the caramel sauce according to the directions on the bottle or jar. Just before serving, peel and thinly slice the bananas.

9 Serve the pavlovas straight from the oven, topped with the warm caramel sauce, sliced banana, cream, and chocolate-dipped salted honeycomb.

Pecan, macadamia, and walnut tartlets

BAKED | PREP + COOK TIME **2 HOURS 15 MINUTES** | MAKES **4**

With their buttery almond pastry filled to the brim with a sweet, treacly mixture of pecans, macadamias, and walnuts, these tartlets are a nut-lover's dream. Make sure that the nuts you use are fresh, so that the filling is as crunchy and flavourful as possible.

1¼ cups (185g) plain flour

⅓ cup (45g) icing sugar

¼ cup (30g) ground almonds

125g cold butter, coarsely chopped, plus extra for greasing

1 egg yolk

filling

⅓ cup (55g) toasted macadamias

⅓ cup (35g) toasted pecans

⅓ cup (40g) toasted walnuts

2 tbsp light soft brown sugar

1 tbsp plain flour

40g butter, melted

2 eggs

¾ cup (180ml) pure maple syrup

1   Process the flour, sugar, and ground almonds with the cold butter until combined. Add the egg yolk and process until the ingredients just come together. Knead the dough on a floured work surface until smooth. Wrap in cling film; refrigerate for 30 minutes.

2   Grease four 10cm loose-bottomed fluted mini tart tins. Divide the pastry into 4 equal portions. Roll out each portion between sheets of baking parchment until large enough to line the tins. Lift the pastry into the tins. Press into the base and side of each one; trim the edges. Cover, then refrigerate for 1 hour.

3   Preheat the oven to 200°C (180°C fan/400°F/Gas 6).

4   Place the tins on a baking tray. Line each pastry case with baking parchment; fill with dried beans or rice. Bake blind for 10 minutes. Remove the parchment and beans. Bake the pastry cases for a further 7 minutes or until lightly browned. Allow to cool.

5   Reduce the oven temperature to 180°C (160°C fan/350°F/Gas 4).

6   To make the filling, combine all the ingredients in a medium bowl. Spoon into the pastry cases.

7   Bake the tartlets for about 25 minutes. Allow to cool.

Almond and apricot filo tarte Tatin

BAKED | PREP + COOK TIME **50 MINUTES** | SERVES **4**

Using canned fruit is a quick way of making this variant of the impressive French dessert, as opposed to the traditional tarte Tatin where the apples are baked before being topped with the pastry. It speeds up the cooking time, which always helps!

10g butter

⅓ cup (75g) firmly packed brown sugar

1 vanilla pod, split lengthways, seeds scraped

4 sheets of filo pastry (thawed if frozen)

825g canned apricot halves in juice, drained

2 tbsp flaked almonds

extra virgin olive oil cooking oil spray

extra thick double cream, to serve

1 Preheat the oven to 200°C (180°C fan/400°F/Gas 6).

2 Combine the butter, sugar, vanilla pod and seeds, and 2 tablespoons water in a medium ovenproof frying pan (base measurement 25cm) over a medium heat. Cook, stirring, for 1 minute or until the butter is melted and the sugar is dissolved.

3 Increase the heat to high. Cook, stirring occasionally, for 2 minutes or until the liquid has thickened slightly.

4 Meanwhile, put 1 sheet of filo pastry on a clean work surface. Spray with the olive oil cooking spray. Top with another pastry sheet, in a cross pattern. Spray with the olive oil. Top with another pastry sheet, placing it diagonally over the last one. Spray again with the olive oil. Top with the remaining pastry sheet, in the opposite diagonal direction. Spray with the olive oil.

5 Arrange the apricots in the frying pan with the sauce, covering the bottom of pan but leaving a slight border; sprinkle over the nuts. Place the pastry, sprayed-side up, over the apricots; carefully tuck in the pastry all the way around the edge of the pan.

6 Bake for 20 minutes or until the pastry is golden and crisp. Carefully turn out onto a serving plate. Cut into wedges, discarding the vanilla pod. Serve warm with thick cream for dolloping over the top.

TIP

Serve with vanilla ice cream or thick Greek-style yogurt instead of the double cream, if you like.

SPICES
AND HERBS

Refreshing, fragrant, soothing, warming,
earthy, exotic – look no further than these
aromatic, tempting treats when you need
a little spice in your life.

Caramel ginger puddings with butterscotch sauce

BAKED | PREP + COOK TIME **1 HOUR** | SERVES **6**

With its indulgent butterscotch sauce and double dose of warming ginger, this inviting dessert is sure to satisfy any sweet craving. You can also make the elements of the recipe ahead of time, then reheat when you are ready to serve (see tips).

1 cup (220g) caster sugar

125g butter, softened

2 tsp ground ginger

2 eggs

$^3/_4$ cup (110g) plain flour, sifted

$^3/_4$ cup (110g) self-raising flour, sifted

$^1/_2$ cup (110g) crystallized ginger, thinly sliced

$^1/_2$ cup (125ml) milk

butterscotch sauce

180g butter, chopped

300ml double cream

$^3/_4$ cup (165g) firmly packed brown sugar

1 Grease 6 holes of a $^3/_4$-cup (185ml) Texas (jumbo) muffin tin. Line the bottoms of the holes with rounds of baking parchment.

2 Put $^1/_2$ cup (110g) of the caster sugar in a small saucepan over a medium-high heat. Cook, swirling the pan often, for 3 minutes or until the sugar is a deep golden colour. Remove from the heat. Carefully pour in $^1/_2$ cup (125ml) water all at once – the mixture will bubble fiercely. Return to the heat. Cook for a further 3 minutes or until the toffee has mostly dissolved. Allow to stand for 5 minutes.

3 Meanwhile, using an electric mixer, beat the butter, remaining $^1/_2$ cup (110g) sugar, and ground ginger in a small bowl until light and fluffy. Beat in 1 egg at a time. Working in 2 batches, fold in the sifted flours and $^1/_3$ cup (75g) of the crystallized ginger, then the milk and cooled toffee.

4 Divide the mixture evenly among the holes of the muffin tin. Bake the puddings for 30 minutes or until a skewer inserted into the centres comes out clean. Turn out onto a wire rack.

5 Meanwhile, to make the butterscotch sauce, combine the ingredients in a medium saucepan. Stir over a medium heat until the butter melts. Bring to the boil. Simmer for 3 minutes.

6 Serve the warm puddings with a drizzle of the butterscotch sauce, topped with the remaining crystallized ginger.

TIPS

• Reheat each pudding for 20 seconds in the microwave before serving. To heat 6 puddings at once, place on a large plate. Microwave on HIGH (100%) for about 2 minutes or until hot.

• The puddings can be made a day ahead and stored in an airtight container.

• The butterscotch sauce can be made up to a week ahead. Keep refrigerated.

• Both the puddings and the butterscoth sauce can be frozen separately for up to 3 months. Thaw both before reheating.

• Serve the puddings with ice cream or thick cream, if you like.

Rose and cardamom soaked doughnuts

FRIED | PREP + COOK TIME **40 MINUTES + STANDING** | SERVES **6**

Soaked in a fragrant rosewater syrup for extra sweetness, and redolent with tastes and aromas of the Middle East, these fluffy bite-sized doughnuts are the dessert of which you've been dreaming. Serve with fresh fruit such as mango, oranges, or strawberries, if you like.

1 tsp (7g) dried yeast

2 egg yolks

3 cups (450g) plain flour

1 tsp ground cardamom

80g butter, softened, chopped

2¼ cups (495g) caster sugar

3 large lemons (600g)

½ cup (125ml) rosewater

vegetable oil for deep-frying

1 Put 1¼ cups (310ml) lukewarm water in a jug. Whisk in the yeast and egg yolks. Put the flour, cardamom, chopped butter, and yeast mixture in the bowl of an electric mixer. Using the paddle attachment, beat for 4 minutes or until the dough is smooth and elastic. Cover the bowl. Allow to stand in a warm place for 1 hour or until the dough has doubled in size.

2 Meanwhile, put 1 cup (250ml) water and 2 cups (440g) of the caster sugar in a small saucepan. Stir over a low heat without boiling until the sugar dissolves. Bring to the boil. Cook for 5 minutes, without stirring, or until the syrup thickens slightly.

3 Remove the zest from 2 lemons using a zesting tool. Juice both of the lemons; you will need ½ cup (125ml) juice. Add the rosewater, lemon zest, and lemon juice to the syrup. Remove from the heat. Cover to keep warm. Finely grate the zest from the remaining lemon. Reserve.

4 Place a wire rack on a baking tray. Fill a large saucepan one-third full with vegetable oil. Heat to 160°C/325°F (or until a cube of bread turns golden in 30 seconds when dropped into the hot oil). Deep-fry heaped tablespoons of the dough, in batches, until lightly browned and cooked through. Drain on the wire rack.

5 Pour the warm syrup over the hot doughnuts. Sprinkle with the reserved lemon zest. Serve immediately.

TIPS

- As you fry, you may need to adjust the heat under the pan to keep the oil at an even temperature.
- Leftover syrup makes a refreshing cordial mixture, or freeze the syrup and make a granita or sorbet.
- You can use orange blossom water instead of rosewater, if you like.

Churros ravioli with chocolate and ice cream

FRIED | PREP + COOK TIME **30 MINUTES** | SERVES **4**

Wonton wrappers are not just for savoury applications. As they are simply flour, eggs, and water, they are a dough that can easily be transformed. Here the wrappers are used to make sweet fried ravioli, given a churros twist with chocolate filling and cinnamon sugar.

24 square or round wonton wrappers (145g)

12 salted caramel chocolate truffles (290g)

vegetable oil for deep-frying

1 tbsp caster sugar

1 tsp ground cinnamon

200g vanilla ice cream

1/2 cup (170g) cherry jam

1 Place 12 wonton wrappers on a chopping board. Working on one at a time, put 1 chocolate truffle in the centre of each wrapper. Brush the edges of the wrapper with a little water. Top with another wrapper; press the edges together firmly (see tip).

2 In a small bowl, combine the sugar and cinnamon until evenly mixed.

3 Heat enough vegetable oil for deep-frying in a medium saucepan over a medium heat until it reaches 170°C/325°F (or until a cube of bread dropped into the hot oil sizzles and browns in 20 seconds). Gently fry the ravioli, in batches, for 1 1/2 minutes or until golden. Remove each batch with a slotted spoon; drain on a tray lined with kitchen paper. Dust with the cinnamon sugar.

4 Put the cherry jam in a small saucepan with 2 tablespoons water. Stir over a low heat until melted and smooth.

5 Serve the warm ravioli with scoops of ice cream and the warmed jam.

TIPS

• Choose your favourite type of chocolate truffles to fill the ravioli.

• You can use marmalade instead of the cherry jam, if you like.

• Make sure that you press out all the air pockets and that the ravioli are completely sealed at the edges; any little gaps will allow melted chocolate to leak out during frying.

• The ravioli can be made to the end of step 1 up to 4 hours ahead of time. Store, covered, in the fridge until needed.

• Any leftover wonton wrappers can be frozen for up to 1 month.

Cardamom and white chocolate crunch

SET | PREP + COOK TIME **20 MINUTES + REFRIGERATION** | MAKES **32**

These addictive confections are perfect for serving as a treat after a meal, or wrapped and presented as a gift. The toasted macadamias and pistachios, in tandem with the tart–sweet mixture of dried fruit, cut through the intense sweetness of the white chocolate.

500g good-quality white chocolate, coarsely chopped

1 cup (35g) rice bubble cereal

1 cup (160g) sultanas

1 cup (155g) macadamias, toasted, coarsely chopped

1 cup (150g) finely chopped dried apricots

1 cup (145g) dried sweetened cranberries

3/4 cup (110g) pistachios, toasted, coarsely chopped

1 tsp ground cardamom

1   Grease a 20cm x 30cm rectangular cake tin. Line the bottom and long sides with baking parchment, extending the parchment 5cm over the sides, to make a sling for lifting the finished crunch out of the tin.

2   Melt the white chocolate in a large heatproof bowl over a large saucepan of simmering water (do not allow the water to touch the base of the bowl). Remove from the heat. Quickly stir in the remaining ingredients.

3   Press the mixture firmly into the prepared tin. Refrigerate for 2 hours or until firm. Cut into squares to serve.

Roast peach and star anise tart

BAKED | PREP + COOK TIME **1 HOUR 15 MINUTES** | SERVES **6**

This striking-looking tart has few ingredients, but it is still a feast for the senses. You can use other fresh stone fruit in this recipe such as nectarines, plums, or apricots. Just remember to choose from the best seasonal produce available and use fruit that is just ripe.

8 small yellow peaches (920g)

1 vanilla pod

20g unsalted butter, chopped

5 star anise

¼ cup (55g) caster sugar, plus extra 2 tbsp

1 sheet of frozen shortcrust pastry, just thawed

1¼ cups (300g) fresh soft ricotta

1 Preheat the oven to 200°C (180°C fan/400°F/Gas 6). Grease a 23cm round pie dish. Line with baking parchment.

2 Cut 6 of the peaches in half; remove the stones. Split the vanilla bean lengthways, then cut in half crossways. Put the peach halves, vanilla pod pieces, and chopped butter in a large bowl with the star anise and the ¼ cup (55g) caster sugar. Toss well to combine. Transfer to a roasting pan. Roast for 20 minutes or until the peaches are tender.

3 Meanwhile, ease the pastry into the prepared pie dish. Prick the base all over with a fork. Cover. Refrigerate for 20 minutes.

4 Remove the peaches from the roasting pan. Put the cooking juices, vanilla bean pieces, and star anise in a small saucepan. Bring to the boil. Cook for 5 minutes until reduced and syrupy. Set aside.

5 Place the pie dish on a baking tray. Line the pastry with baking parchment. Fill with dried beans or rice. Bake blind for 20 minutes. Remove the parchment and beans. Bake for a further 5 minutes or until pale golden in colour.

6 Meanwhile, process the ricotta and the extra 2 tablespoons caster sugar until combined.

7 Spread the ricotta mixture into the pastry case. Arrange the roasted peach halves on top. Bake the tart for 10 minutes or until the pastry is golden and the filling is heated through. Thinly slice the remaining 2 peaches.

8 Serve the tart topped with the slices of fresh peach, drizzled with the star anise syrup.

TIPS

- Make sure to choose peaches that are just ripe.
- You could also make the tart in an 11cm x 35cm loose-bottomed rectangular tart tin. You will need 2 sheets of shortcrust pastry and may need to trim them to fit.
- Before serving, sprinkle the tart with a handful of roasted pistachios, hazelnuts, or pine nuts.
- Use 1 teaspoon vanilla bean paste instead of the vanilla pod, if you like.

Spiced coconut rice pudding with saffron pears

STOVETOP | PREP + COOK TIME **1 HOUR** | SERVES **4**

Although the rice pudding can be served at room temperature, it is at its best when served immediately, fresh, fragrant, and warm. Choose just-ripe pears for this dish, as they will hold their shape and have a better texture after poaching.

³/₄ cup (150g) arborio rice

2 cups (500ml) almond and coconut milk

¹/₂ cup (125ml) coconut cream, plus extra ¹/₃ cup (80ml)

¹/₄ cup (55g) caster sugar

2 fresh bay leaves

1 tsp sea salt flakes

¹/₃ cup (15g) flaked coconut, toasted

saffron pears

¹/₂ cup (110g) caster sugar

¹/₂ tsp saffron threads

2 star anise

3 green cardamom pods, bruised (see tips)

4 small pears such as Anjou, Bartlett, or Concorde (400g), peeled, halved, cored

1 To make the saffron pears, stir the sugar and 3 cups (750ml) water in a medium saucepan over a medium heat until the sugar dissolves. Bring to a simmer. Add the spices and pears, making sure that the pears are fully immersed in the liquid. Reduce the heat to low. Poach the pears for 20 minutes or until tender; remove with a slotted spoon. Return the poaching liquid to the heat. Boil for 10 minutes or until the liquid is a syrupy consistency. Set aside to keep warm.

2 Meanwhile, to make the coconut rice, put the rice, milk, the ¹/₂ cup (125ml) coconut cream, and sugar in a deep non-stick medium saucepan over a medium heat. Cook, stirring, until the mixture comes to a simmer. Stir in the bay leaves. Reduce the heat to low. Cook for 25 minutes or until the rice is just cooked. Stir in the salt flakes.

3 Divide the pudding evenly among 4 serving bowls. Top each serving with a little of the extra ¹/₃ cup (80ml) coconut cream, a poached pear with some of the saffron syrup, and a sprinkling of the flaked coconut.

TIPS

- If the pears are very small, keep them whole and core from the base using a melon baller.
- If you have time, you can poach the pears a day ahead. This will intensify the flavour and colour.
- You can use ¹/₄ teaspoon ground turmeric instead of the saffron, if you like.
- To bruise the cardamom, strike the pods lightly with a rolling pin or pestle. Do not grind or break them. The seeds inside are edible; the pods are not.
- For a twist on the saffron pears, replace the saffron with a small halved red beetroot for pinkish pears.

Black pepper panna cotta with strawberry and basil granita

SET | PREP + COOK TIME **55 MINUTES + REFRIGERATION + FREEZING** | SERVES **6**

Black pepper may not immediately spring to mind when you think of desserts, but it pairs particularly well with strawberries. It is used here in the creamy panna cotta, and its warm, floral, and spicy notes complement the sweet acidity of the strawberry and basil granita.

1 cup (30g) fresh basil leaves

1 cup (220g) caster sugar

250g strawberries, plus extra, sliced, to serve (optional)

3 titanium-strength gelatine leaves (15g) (see tips)

1 cup (250ml) milk

600ml double cream

2 tsp freshly ground black pepper (see tips)

TIPS

• Leaf gelatine comes in different strengths (titanium, bronze, gold, and platinum.) Titanium works perfectly for panna cotta and can be found in the baking aisle of supermarkets.
• The granita can be made a day ahead.
• Serve with shortbread biscuits, almond bread, or other ready-made biscuits or wafers.
• Use 2 teaspoons vanilla extract instead of the black pepper, if you like.

1 Reserve ¼ cup (5g) of the smaller basil leaves to serve.

2 To make the granita, put the remaining ¾ cup (25g) basil in a small saucepan with ¾ cup (165g) of the caster sugar and 2¼ cups (560ml) water. Cook, stirring, over a medium heat without boiling until the sugar dissolves. Bring to a simmer. Cook for 8 minutes. Allow to cool slightly.

3 Trim the tops from the strawberries. Put the strawberries in a food processor. Pour the syrup through a fine sieve over the strawberries. Discard any solids. Process until smooth and combined. Pour the strawberry mixture into a 20cm x 30cm shallow rectangular cake tin. Freeze the granita for 1 hour.

4 Using a fork, break up any ice crystals in the granita. Freeze for a further 3 hours, scraping with a fork every hour, until frozen.

5 Meanwhile, put the gelatine in a medium bowl of cold water. Soak for 5 minutes or until softened. Remove. Squeeze out any excess water. Set aside.

6 To make the panna cotta, put the milk, cream, remaining ¼ cup (55g) caster sugar, and the black pepper in a medium saucepan over a medium heat. Cook, stirring, until the sugar dissolves and the mixture is warm but not simmering. Remove the pan from the heat. Add the soaked gelatine and stir until dissolved. Strain the panna cotta mixture into a jug. Cover the surface directly with cling film. Refrigerate for 30 minutes.

7 Stir the panna cotta mixture. Pour into six 150ml serving glasses. Cover. Refrigerate for 3 hours or until set.

8 Serve the panna cotta topped with spoonfuls of the granita, extra sliced strawberries, and the reserved small basil leaves. Serve immediately.

Panna cotta variations

With a name meaning 'cooked cream' in Italian, panna cotta has a subtlety of flavour and a smooth, silky texture that both take well to being used as a base for other, more dominant ingredients and flavour combinations, as in the recipes below.

Dark chocolate

Make the panna cotta mixture as on page 134, omitting the black pepper; reduce the cream to 300ml and add an extra $1/2$ cup (125ml) milk. Melt 100g chopped dark chocolate (70% cocoa); stir the melted chocolate into the panna cotta mixture until smooth. Continue with the recipe. Serve the panna cotta topped with extra pieces of dark chocolate.

Zesty lime

Make the panna cotta mixture as on page 134, omitting the black pepper and adding 2 tablespoons finely grated lime zest to the cream mixture. After adding the gelatine, strain the mixture to remove the lime zest. Stir in 1 tablespoon lime juice. Continue with the recipe. Thinly peel the zest from 1 lime, avoiding white pith; cut into long, thin strips. Serve the panna cotta drizzled with honey, topped with the strips of lime zest.

Raspberry and rose

Make the panna cotta mixture as on page 134, omitting the black pepper. Purée 100g thawed frozen raspberries. Push the purée through a fine sieve to remove any seeds. Add the sieved purée to the panna cotta mixture with $1/2$ teaspoon rosewater; stir well to combine. Continue with the recipe. Serve the panna cotta topped with extra raspberries and edible dried rose petals.

Eggnog

Make the panna cotta mixture as on page 134, omitting the black pepper and adding $1/4$ teaspoon each of ground nutmeg and ground cinnamon to the cream mixture. Stir in 1 tablespoon brandy. Continue with the recipe. Serve the panna cotta topped with a few pieces of cinnamon stick and a dusting of cinnamon and nutmeg.

Mandarin, honey, and coriander seed cake

BAKED | PREP + COOK TIME **1 HOUR 30 MINUTES** | SERVES **10**

While usually reserved for savoury cooking, herbs actually work very well in sweet cooking.
The unique lemon-like flavour of coriander sweetened with sugar tickles the taste buds.
Its use here intensifies the distinctively floral notes of citrus and honey.

4 mandarins (800g) (see tips)

$^1/_4$ cup (20g) coriander seeds

300g butter, softened

$^2/_3$ cup (140g) caster sugar, plus extra $^3/_4$ cup (165g)

$^2/_3$ cup (230g) runny honey, plus extra $^1/_2$ cup (175g)

4 eggs

1$^1/_3$ cups (200g) wholemeal spelt flour, sifted

2 tsp baking powder

1$^1/_3$ cups (135g) hazelnut meal

1 cup (240g) soured cream

2 tbsp olive oil

1$^1/_2$ cups (375ml) fresh mandarin juice (see tips)

3 sprigs of lemon thyme

3 tsp orange blossom water

Greek-style yogurt, to serve

1 Put 1 whole mandarin in a small saucepan with enough water to cover. Bring to the boil over a medium heat. Reduce the heat to low. Cook, covered, for 30 minutes or until soft. Drain. When cool enough to handle, cut the mandarin into quarters, then remove the seeds. Process in a small food processor until smooth. Set aside.

2 Preheat the oven to 180°C (160°C fan/350°F/Gas 4). Grease a 24cm springform cake tin. Line the bottom and side with baking parchment.

3 Finely grate the zest from 2 of the remaining mandarins; you will need 1 tablespoon zest. Use a zester to remove the zest from the remaining mandarin in long, thin strips. Peel all the mandarins. Cut each into 3 rounds. Put in a heatproof bowl. Dry-fry the coriander seeds in a small frying pan over a medium-low heat until fragrant and lightly toasted. Lightly crush using a mortar and pestle. Remove 2 tablespoons; reserve for the syrup. Pound the remaining seeds until finely crushed.

4 Using an electric mixer, beat the butter and $^2/_3$ cup (140g) sugar until light and fluffy. Add the finely grated mandarin zest, finely crushed seeds, and the $^2/_3$ cup (230g) honey. Beat until well combined. Add the eggs, one at a time, beating well between additions. Working in 2 batches, fold in the combined sifted flour, baking powder, and hazelnut meal, then the soured cream, olive oil, and mandarin purée. Pour into the lined tin; smooth the surface. Bake for 1 hour, covering with foil if browning too much, or until a skewer inserted into the centre of the cake comes out clean. Leave in the tin.

5 Meanwhile, put the mandarin juice, extra $^3/_4$ cup (165g) sugar, extra $^3/_4$ cup (165g) honey, thyme, strips of zest, and reserved lightly crushed seeds in a medium saucepan. Stir over a medium heat until the sugar is dissolved. Simmer for 5 minutes; stir in the orange blossom water. Prick the cake, still in the tin, all over with a fine skewer. Pour 1 cup (250ml) of the hot syrup over the cake. Pour the rest over the mandarin slices. Allow to cool. Serve the cake with the sliced mandarins in syrup and yogurt.

TIPS

• You will need about 8 mandarins for this recipe (including for juice). Look for a seedless variety, or use tangerines or clementines instead, if you like.

• You could also serve the cake with extra double cream or labneh, if you like.

Ginger, rhubarb, and pear lattice tart

BAKED | PREP + COOK TIME 1 HOUR 40 MINUTES + REFRIGERATION, FREEZING + COOLING | SERVES 12

Weaving a classic pastry lattice on top of this tart creates an impressive visual appeal, especially with the ruby-red fruit filling peeking out from below. It is not as difficult to do as it looks, though. Under-and-over repetition is the key action.

3³/₄ cups (560g) plain flour

1 cup (220g) caster sugar

375g cold butter, chopped, plus extra for greasing

2 egg yolks

2 tbsp chilled water

1 egg, lightly beaten

¹/₄ cup (55g) demerara sugar

rhubarb and pear filling

750g trimmed rhubarb stalks, chopped

2 pears (380g), peeled, cut into 2cm pieces

¹/₃ cup (75g) caster sugar

¹/₄ cup (55g) crystallized ginger, chopped

1¹/₂ tsp vanilla bean paste

TIPS

• The rhubarb and pear filling can be made up to 2 days ahead. Refrigerate in an airtight container until needed.

• The pastry can be made 1 day ahead. Refrigerate the portions wrapped in cling film.

• After baking, allow the pie to cool completely before removing it from the tin.

1 Preheat the oven to 180°C (160°C fan/350°F/Gas 4). Grease a 26.5cm (top measurement), 23cm (base measurement), 5cm deep loose-bottomed fluted tart tin.

2 To make the filling, put the rhubarb, pears, and sugar in a baking dish. Roast for 30 minutes. Transfer to a medium saucepan. Cook, stirring, over a high heat for 5 minutes or until thick. Allow to cool. Stir in the ginger and vanilla bean paste. Cover; refrigerate until needed.

3 Meanwhile, pulse the flour, caster sugar, and butter in a food processor until the mixture resembles coarse crumbs. Add the egg yolks and chilled water. Pulse until the pastry just comes together. Knead gently on a lightly floured surface. Divide into two-third and one-third portions. Form each into a disc. Wrap in cling film. Refrigerate for 30 minutes.

4 Roll out the larger portion of pastry between sheets of baking parchment until 3mm thick. Lift the pastry into the tart tin. Ease into the side; trim edge. Prick the bottom all over with a fork. Cover. Freeze for 10 minutes.

5 Place the tart tin on a baking tray. Line the pastry with baking parchment, then fill with dried beans or rice. Bake for 20 minutes or until the edges are crisp and base is half-cooked. Carefully remove the paper and beans. Bake for a further 10 minutes until the pastry is golden and crisp. Cool.

6 Roll out the remaining pastry between sheets of baking parchment into a 25cm x 35cm rectangle. Using a ruler and a sharp knife, cut 12 x 2cm wide, 25cm long strips. Slide the parchment with the pastry strips onto a tray. Cover; refrigerate until needed.

7 Spoon the filling into the tart case. Lightly brush the pastry edge with a little beaten egg. Place pastry strips on top of the filling, weaving as you go, to form a lattice; trim the ends. Brush with a little more egg; sprinkle with demerara sugar. Place the tart on an oven tray. Bake on the top shelf of the oven for 25 minutes or until the pastry is golden and crisp. Leave to cool on the tray for 20 minutes; transfer to a wire rack to cool completely.

Coconut, makrut lime, and pineapple syrup cake

BAKED | PREP + COOK TIME **1 HOUR 15 MINUTES + STANDING + COOLING** | SERVES **8**

Makrut lime leaves are quite different in scent and flavour from ordinary lime leaves. Their flavour is fresh, strong, and somewhat sweet. They are rather tough, so are usually shredded very finely before adding to dishes or mixtures.

2 fresh makrut lime leaves

1 cup (220g) caster sugar

150g butter, softened, plus extra for greasing

3 eggs

1/2 cup (120g) soured cream

1 1/2 cups (225g) self-raising flour, sifted

1 cup (90g) desiccated coconut

1/2 small ripe topless pineapple (450g), peeled, thinly sliced

toasted shredded coconut, to serve

lime cheeks, to serve (optional)

makrut lime syrup

8 large fresh makrut lime leaves (see tips)

1 1/3 cups (300g) caster sugar

2/3 cup (160ml) lime juice

1 Preheat the oven to 160°C (140°C fan/325°F/Gas 3). Grease a 12cm x 23cm loaf tin. Line the bottom and long sides with baking parchment, extending the parchment 5cm over the sides.

2 Remove the makrut lime leaves from the stems; discard the stems. Put the leaves and 1/4 cup (55g) of the caster sugar in a small food processor: process until very finely ground.

3 Using an electric mixer, beat the butter, lime-leaf sugar, and remaining sugar in a small bowl until light and fluffy. Beat in the eggs, one at a time, then the soured cream. Stir in the sifted flour and coconut. Spoon the mixture into the prepared tin. Smooth the surface.

4 Bake the cake for 50 minutes or until a skewer inserted into the centre comes out clean. Leave the cake in the tin for 5 minutes before turning out, top-side up, onto a wire rack set over a tray.

5 Meanwhile, make the makrut lime syrup. Coarsely tear half of the lime leaves. Put the torn leaves, sugar, lime juice, and 1 cup (250ml) water in a small saucepan over a low heat. Stir, without boiling, until the sugar dissolves. Bring to the boil. Remove from the heat. Allow to stand for 5 minutes; discard the torn lime leaves. Finely shred the remaining lime leaves (see tips). Stir into the hot syrup.

6 Pierce the top of cake lightly all over with a fine skewer. Pour half the hot syrup evenly over the top and side of the hot cake. Allow to cool.

7 Put the pineapple in a medium bowl. Pour over the remaining hot syrup. Set aside to cool.

8 Serve the cake with the pineapple in syrup, sprinkled with toasted shredded coconut and with lime cheeks for squeezing over, if you like.

TIPS

- Remember to remove the tough centre rib of the lime leaves before shredding.
- Store the cake in an airtight container for up to 3 days or refrigerate for up to 5 days. Warm gently before serving to refresh.
- The makrut lime is grown for its distinctive double leaves rather than its fruit.

Little ginger citrus cakes

BAKED | PREP + COOK TIME **50 MINUTES + COOLING** | SERVES **12**

These little spiced cakes are a great choice for morning or afternoon tea, and such a pretty picture it is almost a shame to eat them – almost. Drizzled with a simple glacé icing, they are a sublime punch of warm, vibrant, citrussy flavour in a small but perfect package.

20g butter, melted

1/3 cup (50g) plain flour

3/4 cup (110g) self-raising flour

1/4 tsp bicarbonate of soda

2/3 cup (80g) almond meal

3/4 cup (165g) caster sugar

1/3 cup (80ml) extra virgin olive oil

2 eggs, lightly beaten

1/3 cup (80ml) strained freshly squeezed orange juice

3 tsp finely grated lemon zest

2 tsp ground ginger

1 tsp lemon thyme leaves

1 tbsp loosely packed lemon thyme tips

lemon icing

1 1/4 cups (200g) icing sugar

about 1/4 cup (60ml) strained lemon juice

1   Preheat the oven to 180°C (160°C fan/350°F/Gas 4). Grease a 12-hole 7cm (1/2-cup/125ml) mini bundt tin with the melted butter. Divide the plain flour evenly among the holes. Turn and tap the tin until each hole is coated in flour; discard any excess.

2   Sift the self-raising flour and bicarbonate of soda into a large bowl. Whisk in the almond meal and caster sugar. Add the olive oil, egg, orange juice, lemon zest, ground ginger, and thyme leaves until just combined. Spoon the mixture into the prepared holes of the mini bundt tin.

3   Bake the cakes for 20 minutes or until a skewer inserted into the centre comes out clean. Leave the cakes in the tin for 5 minutes. Run a palette knife round the edges of the cakes, before turning them out onto a wire rack to cool.

4   Meanwhile, make the lemon icing. Sift the icing sugar into a medium bowl. Stir in enough of the lemon juice to form an icing the consistency of honey (be careful not to add too much lemon juice, as it reacts with the icing sugar fairly quickly). Drizzle the icing over the cakes, and top with the lemon thyme tips.

TIP

If you're worried about your cakes sticking to the tin, rest the hot tin immediately out of the oven upturned on a cooling rack with a damp clean tea towel resting over the top. The steam created will increase the chances of the cakes coming away from the sides of the tin without sticking.

Orange and rosemary labneh tart

BAKED | PREP + COOK TIME **1 HOUR 30 MINUTES + REFRIGERATION + COOLING** | SERVES **8**

Sweet and tangy from the home-made labneh, this simple baked cheesecake is remarkably easy to put together, even allowing for the overnight draining time. A creamy, light-textured filling infused with the flavours of honey and rosemary is the worthy result.

You will need to start this recipe the day before

800g Greek-style yogurt

3 eggs

2 tbsp runny honey

1 tsp vanilla extract

2 tsp finely chopped fresh rosemary leaves

2 cups (500ml) pure apple juice

a sprig of rosemary, plus extra tips, to serve

3 small oranges (540g), thinly sliced

shortcrust pastry

1^1/$_3$ cups (200g) plain flour

2 tbsp icing sugar

150g cold butter, chopped

2 tbsp iced water

1 To make the labneh, line a medium sieve with a piece of muslin or cheesecloth (or a clean, loosely woven cotton cloth). Place the sieve over a large bowl. Spoon the yogurt into the muslin; cover the bowl and sieve with cling film. Refrigerate overnight.

2 The next day, to make the shortcrust pastry, process the flour, sugar, and butter until the mixture resembles breadcrumbs. Add the iced water; process until the pastry just comes together. Shape into a disc. Wrap in cling film; refrigerate for 30 minutes.

3 Grease an 11cm x 34cm loose-bottomed rectangular fluted tart tin. Roll out the pastry on a floured surface or between sheets of baking parchment until large enough to line the tin. Lift the pastry into the tin; press over the bottom and sides. Trim away excess pastry. Prick the bottom of the pastry case all over with a fork. Refrigerate for 30 minutes.

4 Preheat the oven to 200°C (180°C fan/400°F/Gas 6).

5 Place the tart tin on a baking tray. Line the pastry case with baking parchment; fill with dried beans or rice. Bake blind for 10 minutes. Remove the parchment and beans. Bake for a further 10 minutes or until lightly browned. Allow to cool. Reduce the oven temperature to 140°C (120°C fan/275°F/Gas 1).

6 Drain the labneh. In a large bowl, whisk together the labneh, eggs, honey, vanilla, and chopped rosemary. Spoon the mixture into the cooled pastry case. Bake the tart for 25 minutes or until just set. Allow to cool to room temperature. Refrigerate until cold.

7 Meanwhile, put the apple juice and sprig of rosemary in a medium saucepan. Bring to the boil over a medium heat. Add the orange slices; reduce the heat to low. Simmer for 15 minutes until tender. Allow to cool.

8 Just before serving, drain the orange slices and arrange over the tart. Top with the extra rosemary tips.

TIP

To make a glaze for the top of the tart, simmer 1 cup (250ml) of the orange poaching liquid with ^{1}/$_4$ cup (90g) runny honey over a medium heat until the mixture is reduced by half and syrupy.

Crostoli with vanilla custard cream

FRIED | PREP + COOK TIME **1 HOUR + STANDING + REFRIGERATION** | SERVES **6**

Crisp fried pastries consisting of ribbons of dough fried and dusted with sugar, crostoli are traditionally served at Carnevale. Known by various names across Italy, with several regional variations, they are a bite-sized morsel of deliciousness whatever their name.

$^2/_3$ cup (100g) plain flour

$^1/_3$ cup (50g) self-raising flour

$1^1/_2$ tbsp icing sugar, plus extra, sifted, to dust

1 tsp vanilla extract

2 tsp olive oil

1 egg

about 1 tbsp marsala

vegetable oil for deep-frying

250g strawberries, halved

vanilla custard cream

2 cups (500ml) milk

$^2/_3$ cup (150g) caster sugar

4 egg yolks

$^1/_3$ cup (50g) plain flour

$^2/_3$ cup (160ml) double cream

2 tsp vanilla extract

TIPS

- The crostoli chips can be made a day ahead, then stored in an airtight container until needed. Dust with icing sugar just before serving.
- The custard can be made a day ahead. Store it in the fridge until needed. Flavour the custard with orange liqueur, grated orange zest, or finely chopped chocolate, if you like.

1 Make the vanilla custard cream. Warm the milk in a medium saucepan over a medium heat until just below boiling. Whisk together the caster sugar, egg yolks, and flour in a small bowl until smooth. Whisk the hot milk into the egg yolk mixture. Return the mixture to the same pan. Cook over a low heat, whisking continuously, for 5 minutes or until the mixture boils and thickens. Remove from the heat. Cover the surface of the custard directly with cling film. Allow to cool for 15 minutes. Refrigerate for 30 minutes or until chilled. Using an electric mixer, beat the cream and vanilla in a small bowl until soft peaks form. Whisk the cream into the chilled custard until smooth.

2 To make the crostoli, put the flours and the $1^1/_2$ tablespoons icing sugar in a food processor. Process to combine. Add the vanilla, olive oil, egg, and just enough of the marsala to make the ingredients come together. Knead the dough on a floured work surface until smooth. Wrap in cling film. Allow to stand at room temperature for 30 minutes.

3 Cut the dough in half. Working with a piece at a time, lightly flour the dough, pressing with the palm of your hand to flatten slightly. Use a pasta machine with rollers at the widest setting, the rollers dusted with flour. Feed the dough, a piece at a time, through the rollers 4 times, folding the dough in half each time, until you get an even rectangle. Reduce the setting a notch at a time until the dough is 1mm thick. Place on a lightly floured work surface. Use a crinkled-edge ravioli cutter to cut into 5cm x 12cm strips. Make 2 small slits in the centre of each strip.

4 Heat just enough vegetable oil for deep-frying in a large saucepan over a medium heat until it reaches 180°C (350°F). Cook the dough strips, in batches, for 15 seconds on each side or until light golden and crisp. Drain on kitchen paper. Allow to cool.

5 Dust the crostoli with extra sifted icing sugar. Serve with the strawberries and vanilla custard cream.

Sweet polenta with rhubarb and sweet dukkah

BAKED AND STOVETOP | PREP + COOK TIME **35 MINUTES** | SERVES **4**

Traditionally savoury Egyptian dukkah gets a sweet makeover in this delightful dessert of creamy polenta and roasted rhubarb. The crunch and aroma of the nuts, seeds, and spices in the dukkah provide a counterpoint to the tart–sweet rhubarb.

300g trimmed rhubarb
2¹/₂ cups (625ml) milk
¹/₂ cup (125ml) coconut milk
¹/₄ cup (90g) runny honey
²/₃ cup (130g) white polenta

sweet dukkah

1¹/₂ tbsp unsalted hazelnuts
1¹/₂ tbsp pistachios
1 tbsp sesame seeds
3 tsp coriander seeds
2¹/₂ tsp light soft brown sugar
³/₄ tsp ground cinnamon
³/₄ tsp ground cardamom

1 Preheat the oven to 200°C (180°C fan/400°F/Gas 6).

2 Cut the rhubarb into 8cm lengths. Place in a flameproof roasting pan; cover with foil. Roast for 20 minutes or until the rhubarb is soft but still holds its shape (see tips). Carefully transfer to a plate, leaving a piece of rhubarb behind in the pan.

3 Add 2 tablespoons water to the rhubarb in the pan. Mash until the mixture breaks up. Cook over a low-medium heat, stirring, for 1 minute or until the rhubarb breaks down into a sauce consistency. Remove from the heat. Cover to keep warm.

4 Make the sweet dukkah before turning off the oven. Put the nuts and seeds on an oven tray lined with baking parchment. Dry-roast for 5 minutes. Coarsely crush using a mortar and pestle. Allow to cool. Put the soft brown sugar, cinnamon, and cardamom in a small bowl; add the nut mixture. Mix well.

5 Meanwhile, whisk together the milk, coconut milk, honey, and 1 cup (250ml) water in a medium saucepan. Bring to the boil. Reduce the heat to low. Slowly pour the polenta into the pan. Cook, whisking constantly, for 2 minutes or until thick.

6 Divide the polenta evenly among 4 serving bowls. Top evenly with the rhubarb and rhubarb sauce. Sprinkle with the dukkah to serve.

TIPS

- Cooking time for the rhubarb may vary according to thickness and ripeness, so check after 15 minutes; continue to cook only if needed.
- The rhubarb can be cooked the day before. Store in an airtight container, large enough that the rhubarb holds its shape, in the fridge.

Blueberry basil ice cream pops

FROZEN | PREP + COOK TIME **50 MINUTES + COOLING, REFRIGERATION + FREEZING** | MAKES **12**

These ice cream pops are particularly cooling and refreshing on a hot summer day, and the rich purple swirls of blueberry are hard to resist. And although you do need to allow time for cooling and freezing, this is a no-churn ice cream so it cuts down on fuss factor.

You will need 12 ice lolly sticks for this recipe

250g blueberries (see tips)

1½ cups (75g) firmly packed basil leaves, shredded

1 cup (250ml) double cream

1 cup (250ml) milk

4 egg yolks

½ cup (125ml) pure maple syrup

1½ cups (375g) pot-set Greek-style yogurt

TIPS

• Use fresh rather than frozen blueberries for this recipe, as they will give the best colour and flavour to the finished ice cream pops.

• For a different flavour combination, swap the blueberries and basil with raspberries and mint.

• You will need 12 ice lolly sticks. Trim a quarter length off the ends of the sticks so that they are not too long. Or, if you like, omit the ice lolly sticks entirely. Simply set the ice cream in the loaf tin, then scoop to serve.

• If you're not serving the ice cream pops straight away, return the pops to the freezer, individually wrapped in freezer wrap.

1 Put the blueberries and ¼ cup (60ml) water in a small saucepan. Cook, covered, over a medium heat for 4 minutes or until the blueberries release their juices and collapse. Remove the lid. Cook for a further 4 minutes or until thick and syrupy. Remove from the heat. Stir through the basil. Allow to stand until cooled to room temperature.

2 Put the cream and milk in a small heavy-based saucepan. Bring to a simmer over a medium-low heat; do not boil.

3 Process the cooled blueberry mixture until a smooth purée forms. Push through a fine mesh strainer over a bowl; discard the solids.

4 Whisk the egg yolks and maple syrup until thick and pale. Add the warm milk mixture in a thin stream, whisking constantly until combined. Return the mixture to the saucepan over a medium heat. Cook, stirring constantly, for 10 minutes or until it thickens and coats the back of a wooden spoon (you may need to move the pan slightly off the heat to ensure the mixture doesn't boil during this time). Remove from the heat.

5 Put the yogurt in a medium heatproof bowl. Press the custard mixture through a strainer over the yogurt. Whisk until combined. Refrigerate for 30 minutes or until chilled.

6 Grease and line a 1.5-litre (6-cup) loaf tin with baking parchment, extending the parchment 2cm above the edges of the tin. Pour in the chilled yogurt mixture. Drizzle over the blueberry mixture. Using a spatula, gently swirl the blueberry mixture to create a marbled effect. Freeze for 2 hours until the mixture is partially set. Cover the tin firmly with foil. Using the tip of a small, sharp knife, make 12 small, evenly spaced cuts in the foil. Insert the ice lolly sticks through the cuts and into the ice cream. Freeze for a further 4 hours or overnight until firm.

7 To serve, allow the ice cream to stand at room temperature for 5 minutes to soften slightly, then remove from the tin. Use a hot, dry serrated knife to cut the ice cream into 12 even-sized serves. Serve immediately.

Pecan and pear spiced soufflé cake

BAKED | PREP + COOK TIME **1 HOUR 20 MINUTES + COOLING** | SERVES **10**

This is a lovely cake for a special occasion, or when having family and friends around for lunch or dinner. Pears make for an elegant touch to a dessert, particularly firm varieties that hold their shape but intensify in sweetness on cooking.

2 pears such as Beurre Bosc (460g), halved lengthways

²/₃ cup (65g) pecans

4 large eggs

¹/₄ cup (90g) runny honey

1 tsp vanilla bean paste

³/₄ tsp ground nutmeg

¹/₂ tsp ground cinnamon

¹/₄ tsp ground cloves

2 tbsp wholemeal plain flour

1 tbsp cornflour

¹/₄ tsp sea salt flakes

40g butter, melted, cooled, plus extra for greasing

¹/₃ cup (95g) Greek-style yogurt

1 Preheat the oven to 180°C (160°C fan/350°F/Gas 4). Line a baking tray with baking parchment. Grease and line the bottom and side of a 22cm springform cake tin with baking parchment.

2 Place the pears, skin-side up, on a baking tray. Roast for 40 minutes. Meanwhile, place the pecans on another baking tray. Roast on another oven shelf for the last 5 minutes of the pear roasting time. Allow to cool.

3 Process ¹/₂ cup (50g) of the pecans until finely ground. Coarsely chop the remaining pecans; reserve. Cut each pear half into 5 wedges (to make 20 wedges in total). Core, if you like.

4 Using an electric mixer, whisk together the eggs, honey, cinnamon, and cloves for 10 minutes or until ribbons form when the beaters are lifted. Sift the combined flours and sea salt flakes over the egg mixture. Add the ground pecans and melted butter. Using a large whisk, gently incorporate the ingredients into the mixture.

5 Pour the mixture into the prepared cake tin. Bake on the lower shelf of the oven for 20 minutes. Allow t to cool in the tin for 5 minutes (the cake will collapse as it cools), before turning out, top-side up, onto a wire rack to cool completely.

6 Cut the cake into 10 equal slices. Sprinkle with the reserved pecans. Serve 1 cake slice and 2 pear wedges per person, with a drizzle of the yogurt over the top.

TIP

The cake is best made on the day of serving.

SPECIAL OCCASIONS

These desserts stand out. From dinner
parties and casual entertaining to festive
celebrations or the marking a special day,
you can match the dish to the moment.

Chocolate hazelnut ice cream pandoro

FROZEN | PREP + COOK TIME **25 MINUTES + FREEZING + STANDING** | SERVES **10**

Pandoro, an Italian sweet yeast bread with a long history, is traditionally prepared and served around Christmas and New Year, much like panettone. It is usually cooked in a special pandoro tin that gives the bread its majestic conical star shape.

You will need to start this recipe a day ahead

700g purchased pandoro (see tips)

1 cup (330g) chocolate-hazelnut spread

¼ cup (80g) raspberry jam

1 litre (4 cups) salted caramel ice cream (see tips)

¼ cup (40g) icing sugar, sifted

250g raspberries

purchased good-quality thick vanilla custard, to serve, optional

1 Freeze the pandoro for at least 2 hours or until firm.

2 Turn the pandoro upside down on a cutting board. Using a long, thin sharp knife, held at an angle, cut out a 12cm circle from the base of the pandoro. It should have the shape of a wide but shallow cone. Trim off the tip of the cone, so that you are left with a flat round about 2cm thick. Set aside; you will replace it after you fill the pandoro. Still using the sharp knife, continue to hollow out the pandoro as neatly as possible, leaving a wall of at least 2cm all around. (As the pandoro is star-shaped, it will be thinner in some parts and thicker in others.) Remove the centre of the pandoro. Reserve the pandoro offcuts for another use (see tips).

3 Use a small palette knife to spread the chocolate-hazelnut spread over the inside of the pandoro. Spoon the raspberry jam into the bottom. Freeze for 30 minutes.

4 Meanwhile, remove the ice cream from the freezer to soften for 15 minutes.

5 Spoon the ice cream into the centre of the pandoro a little at a time. Replace the reserved pandoro round. Cover. Freeze for 4 hours or overnight until firm. Remove the pandoro from the freezer 15 minutes before serving.

6 Dust the pandoro with the sifted icing sugar and serve with the raspberries and custard, if you like.

TIPS

- Pandoro is available especially over the Christmas and New Year period. Purchase one from your favourite speciality grocer or order it online.
- If pandoro is unavailable, you can use panettone instead – just remember it won't have the same signature star shape.
- Use the pandoro offcuts to make trifles, Christmas truffles, or bread and butter pudding.
- We used a salted caramel ice cream with chocolate-coated hazelnuts. Choose your favourite flavour and go from there.

Raspberry and almond trifle

SET | PREP + COOK TIME **35 MINUTES + COOLING + REFRIGERATION** | SERVES **10**

Trifle is a real crowd-pleaser at special occasions or when you are gathered around the table for lunch with family or friends, and any leftovers never seem to go uneaten. Take advantage of the most luscious seasonal berries available to make this traditional classic.

3 x 135g packets raspberry jelly cubes

500g small strawberries

250g raspberries

200g purchased sponge cake or butter cake (page 104), cut into 3cm cubes

1/3 cup (80ml) sweet sherry such as Pedro Ximénez

500g mascarpone

2 x 500g cartons vanilla bean custard (see tips)

600ml double cream

2 tbsp icing sugar

2 tbsp flaked natural almonds

1 Make the jelly according to the packet directions. Pour into a 3-litre (12-cup) glass serving bowl. Cut 250g of the strawberries in half. Add to the unset jelly with half of the raspberries. Refrigerate for 1 hour or until almost set.

2 Put the cake in a medium bowl; sprinkle with the sherry. Toss to coat.

3 Using an electric mixer, beat the mascarpone and custard in a large bowl until soft peaks form. Spoon the custard mixture over the jelly. Top with the sherry-soaked cake.

4 Beat the cream and 1 tablespoon of the sifted icing sugar in a large bowl using an electric mixer until soft peaks form. Spoon the cream over the cake.

5 Serve the trifle topped with the remaining berries and the flaked almonds. Dust with the remaining 1 tablespoon sifted icing sugar.

TIPS

- If making your own butter cake, you can use the recipe on page 104 for Spanish caramel orange cake, halving the quantity, or use your favourite sponge recipe instead. Trifle is also a good way to use up leftover cake before it goes stale.
- We used vanilla bean custard, but you can use any good-quality thick dairy custard you like.
- You can use orange juice or orange-flavoured liqueur instead of the sherry, if you like.
- The trifle can be made 1 day ahead up to the end of step 3. Store, covered, in the fridge.

Christmas pudding ice cream bombes

FROZEN | PREP + COOK TIME **30 MINUTES + STANDING + FREEZING** | SERVES **8**

Elegant enough for any festive table, these bombes definitely fall into the category of dishes where ensuring you use premium ready-made ingredients rewards you tenfold in compliments for the 'chef'. For instructions on how to make one large bombe, see the tips below.

You will need to start this recipe the day before

butter for greasing

300g purchased dark fruit cake
or Christmas pudding, coarsely chopped

2 tbsp liqueur of your choice (see tips)

2 litres (8 cups) good-quality vanilla ice-cream,
softened slightly

1 cup (120g) pecans, toasted, coarsely chopped

orange slices

2 medium oranges (480g)

1/4 cup (90g) runny honey, plus extra,
to serve (optional)

1 Grease eight 1-cup (250ml) jelly or dariole moulds.

2 Combine the cake and liqueur in a large bowl until the liqueur is absorbed. Working quickly, add the ice cream to the bowl with the pecans. Stir until just combined. Spoon the ice cream mixture into the prepared moulds. Freeze for 4 hours or overnight until firm.

3 To make the orange slices, preheat the oven to 160°C (140°C fan/325°F/ Gas 3). Line a large baking tray with baking parchment. Cut the oranges into 4mm thick slices. Brush the slices with the honey. Arrange the slices, in a single layer, on the lined tray. Bake for 45 minutes or until starting to caramelize. Leave on the tray to cool.

4 Just before serving, turn out the bombes onto chilled plates or a platter. Top with the orange slices and extra honey, if you like. Serve immediately.

TIPS

- You can use brandy or an orange, coffee, nut, or vanilla liqueur.
- You can use any sort of mould for this dessert, from fluted glasses to plastic cups. Ramekins, individual pie dishes, or even large wine goblets will all work, as long as they hold about 1 cup.
- For a large bombe, line a 2 litre (8-cup) mould or bowl with 2 large pieces of cling film, extending the plastic 10cm over the side.
- The orange slices can be made 1 day ahead. Store in an airtight container at room temperature, layered with baking parchment to prevent the slices from sticking together.

Eton mess wreath

ASSEMBLED | PREP + COOK TIME **30 MINUTES + STANDING** | SERVES **6**

This is at once a celebratory confection and an easy way to serve dessert to a gathering of family and friends. Modelled on Eton mess with its mix of meringues and summer berries, it raises the bar when it comes to presentation, looking as good as it tastes.

200g raspberries

1 tbsp pure icing sugar, plus extra, sifted, to dust (optional)

290g white chocolate

6 coconut macarons

4 raspberry macarons

4 strawberry macarons

250g small strawberries, halved

200g cherries

25g plain mini meringues

unsprayed edible flowers, to serve (optional)

$3/4$ cup (180ml) double cream, whipped

1 Reserve $2/3$ cup (75g) of the raspberries. Process the remaining 1 cup (125g) raspberries and the icing sugar until puréed. Push the purée through a fine sieve over a small bowl. Cover; refrigerate until needed.

2 Place 2 sheets of baking parchment, slightly overlapping, on a work surface to create a wider sheet. Using a 30cm bowl, trace a round. Using a second 20cm bowl, trace a second round in the centre of the first round. You will now have a template for the white chocolate ring.

3 Stir the chocolate in a heatproof bowl over a saucepan of gently simmering water until melted (don't allow the base of the bowl to touch the water). Using the template as a guide, drop spoonfuls of chocolate inside the borders of the ring; using the back of a spoon, spread the chocolate thickly and evenly to fill the ring. Allow to stand until set.

4 Carefully transfer the chocolate ring to a large serving board or flat platter. Arrange the macarons equally around the ring, scattering with the strawberries, cherries (halve some of the cherries and remove the stones, if you like), and remaining $2/3$ cup (75g) raspberries.

5 Crush the mini meringues over the wreath. Scatter with the flowers, if using. Dust with a little extra icing sugar and drizzle with a little of the raspberry sauce.

6 Serve the wreath with the remaining raspberry sauce and whipped cream in separate bowls.

No-churn almond and honey parfait

FROZEN | PREP + COOK TIME **40 MINUTES + COOLING, FREEZING + STANDING** | SERVES **8**

Made with ricotta and yogurt instead of the usual custard base of cream, eggs, and sugar syrup found in classic French parfait, this simple frozen dessert is a glorious melding of smooth creaminess, nutty crunch, and fragrant honey.

You will need to start this recipe a day ahead

400g fresh ricotta

2 tsp vanilla bean paste

$^2/_3$ cup (230g) runny honey, plus extra, to serve

2 cups (560g) Greek-style yogurt

$^1/_2$ cup (80g) toasted natural almonds, coarsely chopped, plus extra, to decorate

1 Line the bottom of a 10.5cm x 23.5cm terrine or loaf tin with baking parchment, extending the paper over the two long sides.

2 Process the ricotta, vanilla bean paste, honey, and yogurt until smooth. Transfer the mixture to a large bowl. Fold in the chopped almonds. Spoon the mixture into the prepared terrine or loaf tin. Smooth the top. Cover tightly with cling film, then with foil.

3 Freeze for 8 hours or overnight until firm.

4 Wipe the outside of the pan with a warm cloth. Turn out the parfait onto a platter. Drizzle with extra honey and chopped almonds to decorate. Cut the parfait into slices to serve.

No-churn parfait variations

The beauty of a frozen dessert is that it can be made well in advance and brought to the table with the minimum of stress. Use any of these clever parfait variations to bring a refreshing restaurant-quality dish to your dinner party or family celebration.

Smashed blackberry and halva

Make the no-churn parfait as on page 166, omitting the almonds. Fold in $1/2$ cup (75g) pistachio kernels, 200g thawed, mashed frozen blackberries, and 100g crumbled chocolate-swirled halva. Continue with the recipe. Serve the parfait drizzled with $1/2$ cup (160g) blackberry jam, warmed with 2 tablespoons water, and topped with extra fresh blackberries.

Berries and chocolate

Make the no-churn parfait as on page 166, omitting the almonds. Stir in $1/2$ cup (75g) toasted hazelnuts, 100g chopped dark chocolate (70% cocoa), 100g fresh or frozen raspberries, and 100g fresh or frozen halved pitted cherries. Continue with the recipe. Serve with extra raspberries and toasted hazelnuts.

Lemon curd and shortbread

Make the no-churn parfait as on page 166, omitting the almonds. Chop 200g all-butter shortbread biscuits into small pieces. Place in a sieve and shake out any small loose crumbs. Fold the biscuits into the parfait mixture. Stir 300g lemon curd to loosen. Add the lemon curd to the parfait mixture and fold through to partially combine. Continue with the recipe. Serve the parfait with thin slices of lemon.

Black sesame and coconut

Make the no-churn parfait as on page 166, omitting the almonds. Stir in 2 teaspoons sesame oil. Combine with $1/2$ cup (35g) toasted shredded coconut and 1 tablespoon black sesame seeds. Continue with the recipe. Serve the parfait topped with lychees in syrup, lime slices, and strips of lime zest.

Burnt Basque cheesecake

BAKED | PREP + COOK TIME **1 HOUR 5 MINUTES** | SERVES **8**

This crustless cheesecake originated in San Sebastian, part of Spain's Basque region, in the 1990s. The high temperature at which it is cooked creates a 'burnt' caramelized crust around the outside, protecting the interior and as a result keeping it soft, creamy, and light.

500g cream cheese, at room temperature

³/₄ cup (165g) caster sugar

3 eggs, at room temperature

1 cup (250ml) double cream, at room temperature, plus extra, chilled, to serve

¹/₂ tsp sea salt flakes

1 tsp vanilla bean paste

2 tbsp plain flour

1 Preheat the oven to 200°C (180°C fan/400°F/Gas 6). Grease an 18cm springform cake tin. Line the bottom and side with baking parchment, extending the parchment 5cm above the top.

2 Using an electric mixer fitted with a paddle attachment, beat the cream cheese until very smooth. Add the sugar. Beat for 2 minutes or until the sugar is dissolved. Add the eggs, one at a time, beating well between additions. Add the 1 cup (250ml) double cream, salt flakes, and vanilla bean paste. Beat until just combined. Sift the flour over the mixture. Beat on low speed until combined, then on medium speed for 10 seconds or just until smooth. Pour the mixture into the lined cake tin.

3 Bake the cheesecake for about 50 minutes or until dark golden but still wobbly in the centre. Remove from the oven. Allow to cool completely in the tin; the cheesecake will sink on cooling.

4 Serve cut into wedges, with extra cream for dolloping over the top.

TIPS

- Preheating the oven to the right temperature is important; it needs to be hot before the cheesecake goes in, so that the crust caramelizes properly.
- Make sure the cream cheese, eggs, and cream are all at room temperature before combining for the cheesecake; this helps them to blend smoothly.
- The cheesecake is best made on the day of serving, but will keep in an airtight container in the fridge for up to 3 days. Bring to room temperature before serving.

Vincotto crème caramel with cherries

BAKED | PREP + COOK TIME **1 HOUR 20 MINUTES + REFRIGERATION** | SERVES **12**

Six ingredients is all it takes to create a sophisticated dessert to serve friends and family at the end of a special-occasion meal. The vincotto adds a sweet-sour edge to the caramel, a finely honed balance of flavour known as 'agrodolce' in Italian.

1 cup (220g) caster sugar
¼ cup (60ml) vincotto
6 eggs
600ml milk
395g sweetened condensed milk
fresh cherries, to serve (see tip)

1 Lightly grease a 16cm x 26cm straight-sided traybake or rectangular cake tin. Place the tin in a larger roasting pan lined with a tea towel. The roasting pan should be deep enough to allow water to come halfway up the sides of the cake tin.

2 Put the sugar and 2 tablespoons water in a small saucepan over a medium heat. Stir until the sugar dissolves. Bring to the boil, without stirring. Boil for 8 minutes or until golden brown. Carefully pour in the vincotto. Boil for a further 1 minute. Pour the caramel into the prepared cake tin. Allow to cool.

3 Preheat the oven to 150°C (130°C fan/300°F/Gas 2).

4 Whisk together the eggs, milk, and condensed milk in a large jug. Put the roasting pan with the cake tin into the oven. With the door open, carefully and gently pour the milk mixture over the caramel in the cake tin. Pour enough boiling water into the roasting pan to come halfway up the sides of the cake tin.

5 Bake for 1 hour. The mixture should wobble in the centre when gently tapped. Carefully remove the cake tin from the roasting pan. Set aside to cool. Cover with cling film. Refrigerate until completely chilled.

6 Gently run a palette knife along the edges of the cake tin to release the custard from the sides. Invert the crème caramel onto a platter with a lip to catch the caramel. Gently cut into 12 equal pieces. Serve topped with fresh cherries.

TIPS

- You can omit the cherries if you prefer, or serve with other fresh seasonal fruit of your choice.
- The crème caramel can be made up to a day ahead. Keep covered in the fridge until ready to serve.

Prosecco jellies with cherries and berries

SET | PREP + COOK TIME **30 MINUTES + COOLING + OVERNIGHT REFRIGERATION** | SERVES **6**

Using Prosecco for the jelly base adds a modern touch to a classic retro dessert, turning it into one for the grown-ups. Rosé Prosecco is a crisp, aromatic sparkling wine, and its floral notes work particularly well with fresh berries.

You will need to start this recipe a day ahead

750ml bottle rosé Prosecco

2 cups (440g) caster sugar

2 cups (300g) fresh cherries, pitted

8 tsp powdered gelatine

1 cup (250ml) water

500g strawberries

125g raspberries

125g blueberries

cooking oil spray

2 tsp icing sugar, sifted

1 Stir the Prosecco and sugar in a large saucepan over a high heat until the sugar dissolves. Bring to the boil. Add the cherries; reduce the heat to low. Simmer, covered, for 3 minutes.

2 Meanwhile, sprinkle the gelatine over 1 cup (250ml) water in a small heatproof jug. Allow to stand for 1 minute. Put the jug in a medium saucepan of simmering water. Stir until the gelatine is dissolved.

3 Transfer the cherry mixture to a large bowl. Stir in the gelatine mixture. Allow to cool slightly. Refrigerate for 30 minutes or until cooled but not set. Remove from the fridge.

4 Reserve 250g of the strawberries, 10 raspberries, and 2 tablespoons blueberries to serve. Hull and halve the remaining strawberries. Combine with the remaining raspberries and blueberries.

5 Lightly spray six 1-cup (250ml) jelly moulds with oil. Pour 2 tablespoons of the jelly into each mould. Divide a quarter of the berries among the moulds. Refrigerate for 30 minutes or until set. Add the remaining jelly and berries; the moulds will not be full. Refrigerate overnight until set.

6 Turn out the jellies onto 6 serving plates (wipe the outsides of the moulds with a warm cloth first, to help release the jellies). Serve with the reserved sliced strawberries, blueberries, and raspberries, dusted with the sifted icing sugar.

TIP

To make 1 large jelly, increase the amount of strawberries used to 750g in total. Lightly spray a 2.5-litre (10-cup) bowl or mould with oil. Pour 1 cup (250ml) of the jelly into the bowl. Add a quarter of the berries. Refrigerate for 30 minutes or until set. Add the remaining jelly and berries to the mould. Refrigerate overnight.

Honeycomb and hazelnut frozen parfait pudding

SET | PREP + COOK TIME 50 MINUTES + OVERNIGHT STANDING + FREEZING | SERVES 8

This pudding recipe retains all the flavours of a traditional steamed Christmas pudding, but with a refreshing frozen twist. It is spectacular enough to be the centrepiece of a festive meal – at the very least, be sure to serve it at the table for best effect.

You will need to start this recipe 2 days ahead

1 cup (240g) mixed glacé fruit

1/4 cup (60g) glacé cherries

1/4 cup (40g) sultanas

1/4 cup (60ml) brandy

4 large eggs, separated

1/2 cup (80g) icing sugar

1/4 cup (25g) cocoa powder

60g dark chocolate (70% cocoa)

1/3 cup (45g) roasted hazelnuts, coarsely chopped

50g chocolate-coated honeycomb bar, coarsely chopped

2 tsp powdered gelatine

1 tbsp hot water

1 cup (250ml) double cream

180g white chocolate

red currants, to serve

1 Put the mixed glacé fruit into a food processor fitted with a metal blade. Process for 3 seconds. Add the glacé cherries; process for 2 seconds. (The fruit chunks should not be too large, or they will tear the pudding when cutting.) Put the fruit in a medium bowl; add the sultanas. Stir in the brandy. Cover; store in a cool, dark place overnight.

2 Line a 2-litre (8-cup) pudding steamer with cling film, smoothing the wrap to remove as many wrinkles as possible.

3 Using an electric mixer, beat the egg whites in a small bowl until firm peaks form. Gradually beat in the combined sifted icing sugar and cocoa powder. Gradually beat in the lightly beaten egg yolks.

4 Put the dark chocolate in a medium heatproof bowl over a medium saucepan of simmering water. Stir the chocolate until smooth. Allow to cool for 5 minutes. Stir the melted chocolate into the egg mixture. Pour the egg-chocolate mixture over the fruit, mix well. Stir in the hazelnuts and honeycomb chocolate.

5 Sprinkle the gelatine over the 1 tablespoon hot water in a small heatproof jug. Stand in a small saucepan of simmering water; stir until the gelatine dissolves. Allow to cool slightly. Stir into the chocolate mixture.

6 Using an electric mixer, beat the cream in a small bowl until firm peaks form. Fold into the chocolate mixture. Pour the mixture into the lined pudding steamer. Smooth the top. Cover; freeze overnight.

7 Invert the frozen parfait pudding onto a chilled serving plate. Remove the steamer; peel away the cling film. Return to the freezer.

8 Put the white chocolate in a medium heatproof bowl over a medium saucepan of simmering water (don't let the water touch the base of the bowl). Stir the chocolate until smooth. Allow to cool for 5 minutes, then spoon gently over the top of the parfait. Return to the freezer at once, to allow the chocolate to set. Top with red currants to serve.

Florentine-topped fruit cake

BAKED | PREP + COOK TIME **3 HOURS + OVERNIGHT STANDING** | SERVES **20**

The Florentine topping used here adds a wonderful crunchy contrast to the tender cake below, turning this moist fruit cake into a veritable panoply of fruit and nuts. This is definitely a cake worthy of celebrating the festive season.

You will need to start this recipe a day ahead

3 cups (500g) sultanas

1 cup (200g) coarsely chopped glacé cherries

1¹/₂ cups (185g) coarsely chopped pitted dates

³/₄ cup (110g) coarsely chopped soft dried apricots

¹/₂ cup (125ml) brandy

250g butter, at room temperature, plus extra for greasing

1 cup (220g) firmly packed light soft brown sugar

1 tbsp finely grated orange zest

5 eggs

¹/₂ cup (60g) almond meal

1³/₄ cups (260g) plain flour

2 tsp mixed spice

Florentine topping

80g unsalted butter, chopped

¹/₃ cup (75g) firmly packed light soft brown sugar

¹/₄ cup (90g) golden syrup

1 cup (80g) flaked almonds

³/₄ cup (150g) glacé cherries, halved

¹/₂ cup (85g) mixed peel

TIPS

- Substitute the dried and glacé fruits with any of your favourites. Keep the weight/quantity the same.
- The cake can be made up to a month ahead. Store at room temperature in an airtight container.

1 Combine the fruit and brandy in a large bowl. Cover. Allow to stand overnight, stirring occasionally, until the brandy is absorbed.

2 Preheat the oven to 160°C (140°C fan/325°F/Gas 3). Grease a deep 22cm round cake tin. Line the bottom and side with 2 layers of brown paper and 2 layers of baking parchment, extending the papers 5cm above the edge of the tin.

3 Using an electric mixer, beat the butter, sugar, and orange zest in a medium bowl until just combined. Add the eggs, one at a time, beating between additions until combined (the mixture may appear curdled at this stage, but will come together later). Stir the egg mixture into the fruit mixture, then stir in the almond meal and combined sifted flour and mixed spice. Mix well.

4 Spoon the mixture evenly into the prepared cake tin. Tap the tin on the work surface to remove any air bubbles. Smooth the surface with damp fingers.

5 Bake the cake for 1 hour 40 minutes.

6 Meanwhile, to make the Florentine topping, melt the butter in a small saucepan over a low heat. Add the sugar and golden syrup. Cook, stirring, until the sugar dissolves. Remove from the heat. Stir in the almonds, glacé cherries, and mixed peel.

7 Spread the Florentine topping evenly over the top of the cake. Bake for a further 40 minutes or until golden brown and a skewer inserted into the centre comes out clean. (If the Florentine topping starts to brown too much, loosely cover the cake with foil.) Place a piece of baking parchment over the top of the cake, then cover the hot cake tightly with foil. Allow to cool in the tin overnight.

Cherry and amaretti white Christmas log

FROZEN | PREP + COOK TIME **35 MINUTES + FREEZING** | SERVES **8**

This frozen fruit-and-nut-filled dessert is replete with the divine flavours of amaretti biscuits and fresh cherries. Instead of cherries, try another fresh fruit such as blueberries, raspberries, or blackberries – and you don't need to limit its eating to Christmas, either.

You will need to start this recipe a day ahead

150g ginger nut biscuits (see tips)

40g butter, melted

200g fresh cherries

1/4 cup (60ml) cherry liqueur or Amaretto

150g amaretti biscuits, crushed

395g canned sweetened condensed milk

500g crème fraîche

1 tsp vanilla bean paste

1/3 cup (75g) crystallized ginger, chopped (see tips)

1 Grease an 8cm x 33cm (2.25-litre/9-cup) straight-sided loaf tin or terrine mould. Line the bottom and sides with cling film or 2 layers of baking parchment or foil.

2 Process the ginger nut biscuits to fine crumbs using the pulse button. Add the butter and process until combined. Press the crumb mixture evenly over the bottom of the tin. Freeze while preparing the ice cream.

3 Freeze half of the cherries for decoration. Remove the pits from the remaining cherries. Coarsely chop. Put the cherries in a large bowl. Add 1 tablespoon of the liqueur and two-thirds of the crushed amaretti biscuits. Allow to stand.

4 Using an electric mixer, whisk together the condensed milk, crème fraîche, vanilla bean paste, and remaining liqueur in a bowl for 5 minutes or until thick. Gently fold the cream mixture into the cherry mixture. Fold in half of the crystallized ginger. Pour over the biscuit base; flatten the surface. Cover tightly with cling film. Freeze for at least 6 hours or overnight until firm.

5 Remove the ice cream log from the tin. Place on a cold platter. Serve topped with the frozen cherries, the remaining crystallized ginger, and the remaining amaretti biscuits.

TIPS

- We used thin ginger biscuits here. Different brands of ginger biscuits contain varying amounts of butter, so you may need to increase the amount of butter used in step 2 if the crumbs do not hold together.
- You can swap chopped dark chocolate for the crystallized ginger, if you like.
- The ice cream log can be made up to 1 week ahead.

Peach, whiskey, and caramel spiced trifle

SET | PREP + COOK TIME **45 MINUTES + REFRIGERATION** | SERVES **10**

Dulce de leche, the thick caramel made by slowly cooking down milk and sugar until browned and caramelized, is used here in a twist on the traditional trifle. Grilled peaches replace summer berries, while the whiskey syrup and spiced custard give the trifle an autumnal feel.

900g purchased Madeira cake, cut into 3cm cubes

$2/3$ cup (160ml) whiskey (see tips)

$1/3$ cup (120g) runny honey

2 tbsp boiling water

5 ripe peaches (750g), cut into wedges

1 cup (300g) dulce de leche

$1^1/_2$ cups (180g) pecans, toasted, coarsely chopped (see tips)

spiced custard cream

600ml double cream

$1^1/_2$ cups (375ml) purchased thick custard

$1^1/_2$ tbsp honey

1 tsp ground cinnamon

$1/2$ tsp mixed spice

1   Arrange the Madeira cake in the bottom of a 4.5-litre (18-cup) bowl or dish, cutting to fit. Combine the whiskey, honey, and the 2 tablespoons boiling water in a jug. Drizzle $1/3$ cup (80ml) of the whiskey mixture over the cake. Transfer the remaining whiskey mixture to a small saucepan over a high heat. Bring to the boil. Simmer for 12 minutes or until reduced by half. Allow to cool.

2   Heat a chargrill plate (or ridged cast-iron grill pan) over a medium-high heat. Grill the peaches, turning, for 2 minutes or until grill marks appear. Transfer to a tray. Refrigerate the peaches until needed.

3   Meanwhile, make the spiced custard cream. Using an electric mixer, beat the cream in a bowl until firm peaks form. Reserve half of the cream. Fold the custard, honey, and spices through the remaining whipped cream. Cover. Refrigerate until needed.

4   Arrange half of the peaches over the cake in the bowl. Top with the spiced custard cream and reduced whiskey mixture. Reserve $1/3$ cup (80ml) dulce de leche for serving. Drop spoonfuls of the remaining dulce de leche over the custard. Sprinkle with 1 cup (120g) of the pecans. Refrigerate for 15 minutes.

5   Swirl the reserved dulce de leche through the reserved whipped cream. Spoon over the top of the trifle. Top with the remaining peaches and sprinkle with the remaining pecans. Serve.

TIPS

• Use peach or orange juice in place of whiskey and jarred peaches instead of fresh, if you prefer.

• To toast the pecans, spread them on a baking tray. Roast in the oven at 180°C (160°C fan/350°F/Gas 4) for 5 minutes or until golden brown. Alternatively, put the pecans in a heavy-based frying pan; stir over a medium heat until fragrant.

• The trifle can be made up to 6 hours ahead and refrigerated until needed.

Grape and dark chocolate panettone loaf

PREP + COOK TIME **1 HOUR 45 MINUTES + STANDING** | SERVES **10**

Like pandoro, panettone is an Italian Christmas speciality, and its popularity has spread
around the world. Serve this contemporary variation, in the shape of a loaf, sliced and toasted
for a delicious festive breakfast or brunch.

³/₄ cup (180ml) whole milk, lukewarm

2 tsp (7g) dried yeast

1 cup (220g) caster sugar

5 cups (800g) white bread flour

1 tbsp finely grated orange zest

3 eggs

4 egg yolks

180g butter, softened

¹/₄ cup (40g) finely chopped candied orange zest

450g red grapes, separated into small clusters

¹/₂ cup (125ml) sweet sherry such as Pedro Ximénez

¹/₂ cup (125ml) fresh orange juice

200g dark chocolate, coarsely chopped

1 egg white, lightly beaten

2 tbsp demerara sugar

1 Combine the milk, yeast, and 1 tablespoon of the caster sugar in a small bowl. Allow to stand for 5 minutes or until slightly frothy on top.

2 Put the remaining caster sugar, 1¹/₄ cups (200g) of the flour, the yeast mixture, and orange zest in a large bowl of an electric mixer fitted with a dough hook. Mix on low speed for 4 minutes or until smooth and elastic.

3 Add the eggs, egg yolks, butter, and remaining flour. Mix on medium speed for 8 minutes or until smooth, glossy, and elastic. Add the candied orange zest. Mix until just combined. Transfer to a lightly greased large bowl. Cover with lightly greased cling film. Allow to stand in a warm place for 3¹/₂ hours or until doubled in size.

4 Meanwhile, put the grapes, sherry, and orange juice in a small saucepan, ensuring the grapes are covered by the liquid. Bring to a simmer over a high heat. Cook for 3 minutes or until the grapes begin to look glossy. Remove the grapes with a slotted spoon to a heatproof bowl. Continue simmering the liquid for 8 minutes or until syrupy and reduced by one-third. Remove from the heat. Allow to cool.

5 Preheat the oven to 200°C (180°C fan/400°F/Gas 6). Grease a 10cm deep, 11cm x 27cm straight-sided loaf tin. Line with 2 layers of baking parchment, extending the parchment 5cm above the edges of the tin.

6 Turn out the dough onto a clean work surface. Flatten into a 28cm round. Sprinkle evenly with the chocolate. Roll up firmly into a log, tucking the ends underneath. Place, seam-side down, in the lined tin. Brush the top of the dough with the egg white; sprinkle with the demerara sugar. Top with a quarter of the grapes. Allow to stand for 30 minutes until risen.

7 Bake for 30 minutes, then cover with foil. Reduce the oven temperature to 180°C (160°C fan/350°F/Gas 4). Bake for a further 40 minutes or until risen and golden. Cool in the tin for 15 minutes. Lift the loaf out of the tin using the baking parchment; place on a wire rack to cool completely. Serve the panettone in slices with the syrup and remaining grapes.

TIP

Panettone is best eaten on the day or within 2 days of baking. Store any leftover panettone in an airtight container. Leftover panettone can be enjoyed sliced and toasted.

Eggnog bavarois cake

BAKED | PREP + COOK TIME 45 MINUTES + REFRIGERATION + FREEZING | SERVES 10

This is a show-stopper of a cake. We have added a touch of cinnamon, nutmeg, and cloves
to the creamy centre bavarois-style layers, transforming this cake into a festive delight. You
don't have to keep it a seasonal choice, though, as it is hard to resist at any time of year.

500g purchased thick vanilla custard

1/3 cup (80ml) dark rum

1/3 cup (75g) caster sugar

1 tsp vanilla bean paste

1 tsp ground nutmeg

3/4 tsp ground cinnamon

1/2 tsp ground cloves

6 small gelatine leaves (10g)

1 quantity Stacked Mocha Blackout Cake
(see page 82; see also tips)

300ml double cream

chocolate trees

1 cup (150g) dark chocolate melts, melted

2 tsp chocolate sprinkles such as stars, pearls,
and sticks, or 2 tsp gold and silver sugar pearls

gold sanding sugar

rum butterscotch sauce

1 cup (220g) firmly packed soft light brown sugar

300ml double cream

50g butter, chopped

1 tbsp dark rum

TIPS

- The cake and sauce can both be made a day
ahead and refrigerated. If the sauce separates,
stir well to bring it back together before serving.
- Allow the cake and sauce to stand at room
temperature for 45 minutes before serving.

1   Place half of the custard, the rum, sugar, vanilla, and spices in a medium
    saucepan. Bring to the boil, whisking until the sugar dissolves. Simmer
    for 2 minutes. Remove from the heat.

2   Put the gelatine leaves in a bowl of cold water for 5 minutes until
    softened. Squeeze out any excess water from the gelatine; add to the hot
    custard mixture. Stir until dissolved. Transfer to a large heatproof bowl.
    Whisk in the remaining custard. Allow to stand for 5 minutes until cool.

3   Grease a deep 15cm round cake tin. Line the bottom and side with
    2 layers of baking parchment, extending the paper 5cm above the edge
    of the tin. Trim the tops of cakes to level and the side of each cake so that
    it fits the cake tin. Cut each cake in half horizontally. Reserve the
    trimmings until needed. Place a cake layer in the bottom of the tin.

4   Beat the cream in a medium bowl until medium peaks form. Fold in the
    custard. Working quickly, pour 1 cup (250ml) of the custard cream over
    the cake in the tin. Top with another cake layer. Repeat layering with the
    remaining custard cream and cake layers, finishing with custard cream
    over the top. Use a small palette knife to level the surface. Tap the tin on
    the worktop to remove air bubbles. Cover. Refrigerate for at least 4 hours.

5   Meanwhile, make the rum butterscotch sauce. Combine the ingredients
    in a small heavy-based saucepan. Bring to the boil, stirring, until the
    sugar dissolves. Simmer for 5 minutes or until the sauce thickens. Allow
    to cool. Refrigerate until cold and thick.

6   Place 3 skewers or wooden stir sticks on a baking tray lined with baking
    parchment. Put the melted chocolate in a paper piping bag. Snip off the
    end of the bag with scissors. Pipe tree shapes halfway up the skewers.
    Decorate with sprinkles and sanding sugar. Freeze until firm.

7   Remove the cake carefully from the tin. Insert the trees into the top.
    Crumble some of the reserved cake trimmings around the tree 'trunks'.
    Serve the cake with the rum butterscotch sauce.

Conversion chart

A note on Australian measures

- One Australian metric measuring cup holds approximately 250ml.

- One Australian metric tablespoon holds 20ml.

- One Australian metric teaspoon holds 5ml.

- The difference between one country's measuring cups and another's is within a two- or three-teaspoon variance, and should not affect your cooking results.

- North America, New Zealand, and the United Kingdom use a 15ml tablespoon.

Using measures in this book

- All cup and spoon measurements are level.

- The most accurate way of measuring dry ingredients is to weigh them.

- When measuring liquids, use a clear glass or plastic jug with metric markings.

- We use large eggs with an average weight of 60g. Fruit and vegetables are assumed to be medium unless otherwise stated.

Dry measures

metric	imperial
15g	$1/2$oz
30g	1oz
60g	2oz
90g	3oz
125g	4oz ($1/4$lb)
155g	5oz
185g	6oz
220g	7oz
250g	8oz ($1/2$lb)
280g	9oz
315g	10oz
345g	11oz
375g	12oz ($3/4$lb)
410g	13oz
440g	14oz
470g	15oz
500g	16oz (1lb)
750g	24oz ($1\frac{1}{2}$lb)
1kg	32oz (2lb)

Liquid measures

metric	imperial
30ml	1 fluid oz
60ml	2 fluid oz
100ml	3 fluid oz
125ml	4 fluid oz
150ml	5 fluid oz
190ml	6 fluid oz
250ml	8 fluid oz
300ml	10 fluid oz
500ml	16 fluid oz
600ml	20 fluid oz
1000ml (1 litre)	$1^3/4$ pints

Length measures

metric	imperial
3mm	$1/8$in
6mm	$1/4$in
1cm	$1/2$in
2cm	$3/4$in
2.5cm	1in
5cm	2in
6cm	$2^1/2$in
8cm	3in
10cm	4in
13cm	5in
15cm	6in
18cm	7in
20cm	8in
22cm	9in
25cm	10in
28cm	11in
30cm	12in (1ft)

Oven temperatures

The oven temperatures in this book are for conventional ovens; if you have a fan-forced oven, decrease the temperature by 10–20 degrees.

	°C (Celsius)	°F (Fahrenheit)
Very slow	120	250
Slow	150	300
Moderately slow	160	325
Moderate	180	350
Moderately hot	200	400
Hot	220	425
Very hot	240	475

Index

Acknowledgments

DK would like to thank Sophia Young, Joe Reville, Amanda Chebatte, and Georgia Moore for their assistance in making this book.

The Australian Women's Weekly Test Kitchen in Sydney has developed, tested, and photographed the recipes in this book.